ABOUT FAMOUSLY HELPFUL

Marketing as we know it is history.

It doesn't matter if you're pitching for a new job, filling seats at a benefit or selling an amazing new product, the world is too cluttered for your message without spending millions on advertising.

The old system is dead, but radical change creates a fleeting window of opportunity for those who are willing to change themselves.

Successful marketers of tomorrow are flipping the rules upside down. This new era has abandoned self-promotion and hype for an others-centered approach. In today's economy, marketing starts with helping.

There is no better way to grow, no better way to cut through the hot mess, no better way to reach your audience than to help them. Become famous for your helpfulness and watch how your life changes. You might never have to look for another customer, donor, or job again.

FAMOUSLY HELPFUL: THE SURPRISING RESULTS OF FLIPPING SELF-PROMOTION, HYPE AND MARKETING UPSIDE DOWN

Library of Congress Cataloging-in-Publication Data Available

ISBN-13 978-1519201287

ISBN-10 1519201287

Cover illustration and design by Justin Blaney

First edition: March, 2015

10 9 8 7 6 5 4 3 2 1

www.justinblaney.com

An *Inkliss* Book

To all who have taught me about helping by example. This book wouldn't exist without you.

Famously Helpful

The surprising results of flipping
self-promotion, hype and marketing upside down

JUSTIN BLANEY

CONTENTS

MARKETING WILL NEVER BE THE SAME

I'll never forget something Rick Wong told me the first time I met him. Rick is a middle-aged sales expert who has experience running major divisions at Microsoft and Hewlett Packard and even earned quarterly meetings with Michael Dell for a season. When I met him, he'd recently launched a consulting firm to help others with their careers and he was writing a book. After hearing him speak at an event, I reached out and he was gracious enough to meet.

We sat at a round table in a strip mall suburban Seattle Starbucks, the flagship variety that comes with a Clover machine and hordes of middle school kids at around three in the afternoon. We were wrapping up with a sort of get to know you meeting when a thought occurred suddenly to Rick.

"You should meet Lisa Hufford, you'd love her! She runs an enormously successful consulting firm that's about to break $50 million in revenue, and she's only been at it a few years." Rick leaned toward me as if he was about to share the secret to his grandmother's cookie recipe. "Lisa is so successful because she loves helping people."

Something I've learned about Rick as I've gotten to know him is that he lives by the same principles that he ascribed to Lisa, which is probably why the two of them run in the same circle. People like Rick and Lisa achieve a disproportionate amount of success because, in part, of their willingness to help others. This willingness has caused them to acquire influential friends, people willing to do anything for them, and a small army of advocates who recommend them whenever the opportunity arises. I've seen, not just in Rick and Lisa but in hundreds of others, that this helpful spirit is often correlated with success in business and, to the point of this book, sales and marketing.

We need to pause here and consider something. There are a lot of misconceptions about marketing and its role. When I was first starting out in business, I misunderstood marketing because of what I was learning from other business people, in business school and from the dozens of books I read on marketing. Observation has shown that many of the things I was taught are actually myths. Here are a few examples:

Marketing is important no matter the outcome. I've learned that marketing is actually worthless if it doesn't result in increased sales.

Good marketing can increase sales for any company. Observation has shown that marketing is just one small piece of business success and if the other areas, like quality, service, business model, industry, niche, staff and leadership are out of sync, marketing will produce few, if any, results.

Companies can't succeed without good marketing. I've seen firsthand how many companies can do little to no marketing—and what marketing they do is atrocious—and still manage to achieve enormous success.

Networking isn't marketing. I've come to see networking (a much expanded definition of networking, as we'll explore later) as an important part of marketing for many companies and one of the easiest and least costly methods for improving sales.

Success in business is all about who you know. I've learned that it's far more important to consider who knows you.

So what is marketing anyway?

Marketing is a means for introducing You to someone else. You could be your service or product, an organization or business or, well, You could be you. Marketing unlocks the principle that it's all about who knows You. The most well-known, most traditional marketing methods such as television or outdoor advertising are all about getting a message in front of more people so the public will know about a product or service. These methods rely on sending the same message so often that the consumer will know one brand better than any other and that they'll select that brand when the time comes. This is all about being known for a certain niche and being known more than your competitors. BMW is known for being a fun car to drive and it's known more than Alfa Romeo because, among other factors, of the volume of advertising over time.

The problem is, marketing is broken.

The world is too cluttered for most of us to use traditional marketing. We're all bombarded with emails, advertisements, phone calls and even people flipping signs on the street corner. We've been taught for the last century that marketing is all about blasting a message through a bullhorn and, as more people have started blasting their messages, most of us have simply tried to find a louder bullhorn. Or we make our message more annoying so people remember it (we all have a fond place in our hearts for those local appliance store ads, right?). But what happens when we can't find a louder bullhorn? Or we can't afford one? And even if we do find a louder bullhorn, the people we're shouting at are tired of all the shouting and self-promotion. The market is jaded to our eye-catching headings and sensational subject lines. They're sick of us talking about us all the time. So they shut down. They don't ever answer their phone unless they recognize the number. They buy program after program to make sure that no spam messages get through. They're subscribed to so many blogs and newsletters now that many have purchased programs that will make it so they don't have to see the newsletters and blog emails they've subscribed to.

So what do most businesses do? Nothing. Or close to nothing. Marketing isn't fun. It's horrible actually, at least in its old school form. Constantly talking about how great we are, trying to pry a few bucks out of someone's wallet with a clever twist of words or a sexed up advertisement that promises the good life in exchange for $39.95. So many companies with great products and services have given up on marketing altogether. They're frustrated with how hard it is to get anyone's attention so they get by on their own momentum, a bit of word of mouth and client referrals. Nonprofits have it even worse, barely scraping by on a few big events each year that increasingly feel like *deja vu* to those who attend. Many businesses, nonprofits and individuals are in this together. They could grow so much and help so many people. Companies with great products and services, nonprofits capable of enormous impact, individuals with something big to offer the world, or at least their next employer, shouldn't have to struggle to get their message out there and attract new customers, donors and opportunities.

There is good news for these businesses.

A growing number of companies, individuals

and nonprofits have discovered the power of becoming known by helping others.

This isn't a new idea. It's been around as long as humans have, it's just that people moved away from these ideas when marketing came on the scene. Marketing is a shortcut to getting your message out and it worked pretty well for a while. Remember when email was new and it was a brilliant idea to blast your message out to as many email addresses as you could grab? Then everyone started doing it and it became spam. What was once a sweet marketing shortcut has now become about as socially acceptable as simultaneously slapping someone in the face and stomping on their toe. So helping is coming back into fashion. Yes it's slow and, in some ways, more difficult. But many have discovered the quiet power of helping. They've pivoted from talking about themselves to talking about others. They've given up hyping their own game and instead are spending their energy serving their target audience selflessly. As a result, their influence and bottom lines have been growing faster than they thought possible, far faster than their competitors who are still relying on strategies used by male enhancement drugs and scam artists claiming to have come into a royal inheritance in Africa.

There is no better way to grow, no better way to cut through the clutter, no better way to reach your audience than to help them. I call it becoming *famously helpful.* I've seen this work for job seekers, sales people, nonprofits, even people looking for a friend. This is about becoming so known for your helpfulness that people flock to you for advice. They line up to buy your books. They sign their friends up for your email list. They retweet everything you say. They buy the products you sell, they donate to the causes you champion and they beg you to come work for them.

This books explores the principles of this approach that's flipping the traditional ideas of marketing, self-promotion and hype upside down and, in the process, making people and organizations famous for their helpfulness.

This is helpeting.

Yes, it's a little bit corny, but it'll grow on you. It's important to distinguish between marketing/self-promotion/hype and the concepts discussed in this book. Having a word to quickly describe this new way of building influence is essential.

So what is helpeting? In many ways it's the opposite of marketing. Where marketing is about self-promotion, helpeting is about promoting others. Where marketing is about spamming people with your message until they remember you, helpeting is about serving people and building relationships that turn into business. Where marketing is about spending as much cash as you can to blast your message across the sky, helpeting is about spending a limited budget carefully, focusing on how to serve your target audience with resources, advice and connections. Helpeting goes beyond merely being known. It's a system for you to serve your target market and become powerfully known by customers without spending millions on advertising. But it's more than that. Helpeting is a tool for increasing trust with an audience who is already aware of you. After becoming known by someone, it's important to continue to help that person in order for your marketing to result in sales. People rarely buy something the first time they hear about it, especially in larger, more complicated purchases like hiring a consultant or selecting accounting software. In many situations, the timing isn't right. The customer might need to wait for their current contract to end or they might not have the budget until January. So if you're introduced to someone and don't build trust over time, your only chance of a sale is if you can close customers in that first moment they hear about you. If that's your business model, this book may not be right for you.

Finally, Helpeting makes it easy for people to understand and buy your product or service. Millions of people may know and trust you, but if they don't realize you have a service that would solve their problem, they'll never buy. Many businesses make the mistake of thinking that people who know and trust them will take the initiative to learn about what they do. That sounds awfully nice, but in my experience it's unrealistic to even expect your family to do this. You know this is a problem at Christmas every year when Uncle Barney asks, "So what have you been up to lately?" which is code for, "I have no idea what you do for a living, but I'm too embarrassed to admit it." If your family can't remember what you do, I guarantee your potential customers won't. So the burden is on you to present your value clearly, concisely and readily. And repetition still counts in helpeting. Even people who don't like you will remember what you do if they hear about it often enough, and with helpeting, the repetition won't come from you obnoxiously spamming people.

To sum it up, there are three steps to increasing sales through helpeting:

1. Become known by helping people

2. Increase trust through consistency over time

3. Make it easy for customers to understand and buy your unique value

Don't be fooled by the simplicity and commonsense of these three principles. They have the power to make you more successful in marketing your company than anything I've encountered in business. Over the following pages we'll explore case studies, research and practical examples of how to implement each of these steps into your business.

PART 1. BECOME KNOWN BY HELPING PEOPLE

IT'S NOT WHO YOU KNOW

Franklin, Tennessee is a bedroom community outside Nashville. It's one of those places that seems to have been forgotten by the twenty-first century. From the town square to the old brick colonials to the quiet way of life, it would be easy to forget that horses aren't the preferred mode of travel for commuters who pick twangy country tunes on Music Row just 15 miles away. My destination was a local legend of pastries and chicken salad on Main Street called Merridee's Breadbasket. I arrived a little early and grabbed a black coffee while waiting for my appointment to arrive.

Jeff Goins is a blogger, writer and entrepreneur who has tapped into the nerve of thousands of dreamers who are working toward becoming authors and, while they're at it, changing the world. He also happens to resemble Luke Skywalker. He arrives and, after taking a selfie with him and posting it on Instagram with the caption, "Can't believe I'm having lunch with @MarkHamilton #maytheforcebewithyou," Jeff and I grab our food and get down to business.

Those of us who wish to build a tribe for the purpose of helping people and otherwise increasing our influence can learn a lot from Jeff. One thing I've learned from him is that it's helpful for web traffic if your blog is listed on a bunch of influential people's sites. Jeff, for example, is cited as a great resource on dozens of blogs from Michael Hyatt (michaelhyatt.com) to Darren Rowse (problogger.net) to Funny Cat Pix (funnycatpix.com). Just another example of it's all who you know, right? This is one of the most commonly cited adages of business success. There's only one problem with this saying. It's wrong. Increasing your influence isn't about who you know. It's about who knows you. And the best way to become known by someone is to help them.

Jeff has built his career on helping people. Through his blogging, his books, his speaking and even his personal connections, he's a servant. When he helps people, they remember him. If they remember him enough, they might put him as a resource on their website, refer a friend, buy his next product or post pictures of him on FunnyCatPix.com, which increases his fame exponentially. It's so easy to forget the power of simple service, untainted by self-interest. Guys like Jeff figured this out at a young age. It takes a little longer for some of us and the majority of people, I'm convinced, never learn this lesson. In order to get what you want from life — love, power, influence, money, popularity, anything really, except good looks—you have to stop striving for that thing you want and start serving others. Serve them with a tweet. Serve them with a hug. Serve them with a couple bucks. Serve them by sharing your platform, no matter how big or small. Serve them by teaching them what you know. Even if you're dumb, find someone who's even dumber. This is one of the great lessons of Facebook or the comments section on ESPN: there is always someone dumber.

Start where you are.

Don't worry about the approximately seven billion people who aren't in your boat. Serve the one sitting next to you. Even if they have body odor. Serve them with a stick of deodorant. Then you're not only serving this one person, but everyone else around you too. See how the exponential power of this principle begins to work for you? If you do this, I can't guarantee that you'll become the next Jeff Goins or that you'll wake up one morning and find that you look like Luke Skywalker or even that you'll have your pictures up on FunnyCatPix.com. I can promise people will know you, and being known is one of the most powerful forces in the universe.

It isn't who you know.

It's who knows you.

One of the best parts of this reversal is that it unlocks incredible potential for growth. There is a limit to the number of people you can know, but literally billions of people can know you. Fame is powerful and it can be used to make your sales grow explosively. It's so simple and logical, it almost seems too obvious. Yet so many companies, small businesses in particular, skip over this important step. People wonder why more seats aren't filled at their annual fundraisers or why they have difficulty launching a new product, a product that was so good it was supposed to sell itself. But people can't buy something they've never heard of.

So how do you become more known? There are some nefarious approaches and some very expensive ones. Both have their down sides. What we need is a system for becoming known, whether it's by a hundred people or a million, that doesn't cost a lot of money. Helping people is the most consistent method I've found, partly because there are a number of laws of human nature at work when it comes to helping others. One is that by helping people you create a sense of indebtedness and people want to reciprocate, not out of guilt but out of genuine caring. Another is simply that by being helpful you separate yourself from 99% of the world. Everyone is trying to get everyone else's attention, especially people who have the power to buy or influence buyers. Being helpful is the opposite of asking for something. If you're able to help someone in a big way, you become something of a hero to them. Consider somebody going through all this grief over some massive headache of a problem and here you come riding in with the answer. You help them solve their problem for a lot less money and with far less complexity than they thought possible, then you just take off without asking for anything in return. There's a nice, mysterious hero ring to that, right?

So the big idea is that you find some way to help someone. There are a number of ways to increase your return on investment from these kinds of activities, but let's start with the simplicity of just helping. You can start, immediately, living a more successful, fulfilled life by having a helpful spirit about you no matter who you're with. Becoming others-centered and ridding yourself of whatever tendencies you have toward self-focus is powerful in and of itself. If you find that helping people is starting to show some results and you want to ramp it up, you can focus on helping the right people, a targeted group of people, in a targeted way. The right people are not just influential people. Ideally, they're your target market. Even more ideally, they're the people responsible for saying yes or no to buying whatever it is your selling. You can increase your results by helping them in the right way. You can help your target customer find flowers for his wife, and that's a great way to make sure he remembers you. However, it's even better to help him in a way that highlights your specific area of expertise. If you're a relationship consultant, helping him find the best flowers might be the very thing to do this. If your field is solutions for project management, there's likely a better way. The later sections in this book have numerous examples and case studies that examine how to put these ideas to work for you.

It's important to remember that the method for becoming known doesn't matter as much as finding and implementing a system that works for you. The examples throughout this book highlight many different angles to help you discover what works best for you on your journey toward being discovered. You might be a best kept secret, but it's time to change that. Or you might already have a large amount of awareness and you simply need more of it. Maybe a lot more. No matter where you're coming from, the same principles work for helping you get to your sales goals. The good news is that, no matter how big you are, chances are the vast majority of the world hasn't heard of you yet, even if you narrowly define your target market. That means we have a lot of upside potential. So let's get to work introducing you to the world in a big way.

YOU DON'T HAVE TO BE GREAT TO HELP SOMEONE

The birth dates of the world's most influential people are often celebrated as holidays. When do you celebrate a person who doesn't know her own birth date? Or even where she was born? That's exactly how Harriet Tubman's story begins. She was born the daughter of a slave, became a slave herself, then went on to become one of the most important figures in American history.

Harriet could not have been born to greater disadvantage. Ruthlessly abused, neglected and ignored, Harriet turned her disadvantages into her strengths. The world wanted to forget her, so she let them, slipping through the cracks of society and then slipping through the night, stealing away forgotten souls and whisking them off to a new world that would never forget her. I love the reminder of how far we can go and how much impact we can have regardless of where we started. We're all captivated by the stories of successful people who started with nothing. But did they really have nothing? Did they have Harriet nothing? If we remember that Harriet Tubman changed the world, having started with so little, we'll find it more difficult to make excuses for ourselves. The simple fact that you're reading this indicates you have at least an elementary education. That one fact puts you light years ahead of Harriet Tubman. Yet she was smart, driven, entrepreneurial and unwilling to settle. As a young slave she negotiated a rare arrangement with her master, effectively becoming her own agent. She hired her services out, paying her master for the right to do so, but keeping a bit for herself. With this money, she began to build her future.

One of the assets she needed was a cow, which cost $40. Harriet figured she could save $10 a year which would allow her to make the purchase after just four years. Can you imagine saving everything you have for four years just to purchase a cow? I have a difficult time waiting two days for my orders to come from Amazon, but Harriet had vision. She had a desire to build something bigger than the moment. Build something she did. Today, hundreds of years later, we're still talking about a slave who fought for her freedom and reminded slaves of their own intrinsic worth, their value as human beings that could not be bought or sold. Harriet made a huge impact on a very difficult period of history, but remember that helping people is about making yourself accountable to effort, not results. There are too many variables in life to guarantee success at anything, and anyone who tells you otherwise is probably trying to sell you something. Helpeting isn't about a guaranteed path toward greatness or riches or power, but it is a system that has been proven time and time again to lead to something better.

It doesn't matter what you start with, you can improve yourself and those around you by focusing not on yourself, but on others.

If Harriet did it, so can we.

APPLICATION FOR TODAY

Write a list of the advantages you have that make it easier for you to help those around you. How can you make better use of those advantages to help people more powerfully? Jot down a few thoughts and save them for later.

CHRISTMAS LIGHTS

There is nothing more magnificent in this world than taking a nap after eating Thanksgiving dinner. However, for many millions of unfortunate moms and dads around the world, there is one task that must be done before the napping can commence: putting up the Christmas lights.

Now that my children are teenagers, I increasingly find myself putting up the lights on my own, but when they were young the hanging of the Christmas lights was the highlight of their Thanksgiving weekend. I can hang the lights on my own in about 30 minutes flat, especially if I know a nice nap on the couch and some Thanksgiving football waits for me in the warm living room. But nothing takes 30 minutes when you have three kiddos helping. Of course, I loved hanging lights with my kids each year, even if they did slow me down and I could hang the lights straighter on my own. Because hanging the Christmas lights wasn't about me working efficiently or about the lights looking perfect. It was about family time.

One lesson that came up year after year during this event was that helping isn't a self-centered thing. Picture your own rosy-cheeked child, or a niece or nephew or grandchild, and how, in the absence of something immediate to do, that cute little face twists into something that resembles a witch crossed with a tomato, and then those fateful words scream out, "I want to help!" This is often followed by, "Suzy is doing it all! It's my turn!" These situations presented me with the opportunity to teach my children that helping isn't about them and that when one person tries to make it all about themselves they ruin family time for everyone else.

Helping is about being useful to

others, not ourselves.

This seemingly obvious point is missed by many people who claim they want to help others when, in reality, they want to help themselves. This is played out in numerous situations including when someone who can't sing wants to help out the church worship band, or when someone who wants a raise helps their boss by staying late (at least when the boss is looking) or when someone wants a favor from their spouse and they help by doing the dishes (again, when the spouse is looking). These examples are illustrations of helping in order to get something in return. Just like the five year-old versions of my children who wanted to help, but really just wanted to do all the fun stuff and make sure that their siblings didn't get to do any of the fun stuff.

Helping that isn't selfless is at best an investment and at worst manipulative and selfish. When you help someone and expect a return on that helping, you're making an investment. Just like when you give your money to the bank and expect them to return it to you with a little extra for your effort. There's nothing wrong with making investments, but it shouldn't be confused with selfless helping that expects nothing in return. The worst form of self-serving help is manipulative. Someone is attempting to covertly get something in return for their "help," something greater than what they've offered, using trickery.

When it comes to increasing your sales success through the principles of helpeting, we realistically should expect a return on our helping investment but we have to be careful about our motivations and expectations. We have to start with pure motives or our results will be diminished greatly. People have a sense for intentions. And successful people, the kind of influential individuals who make the final decision about whether to work with us, are even more adept at sniffing out inauthenticity. You must go into an individual helping opportunity with the desire to help and with no expectation of a return. If you can't do this, helpeting won't work for you. That's not to say you're blind to the need for helpeting to yield a return on your investment over time, but you have to be willing to play the long game. It may seem like a fine line distinction, but it makes all the difference. If you're just starting out with helpeting, start by helping those in your life with no intention of receiving anything from them, ever. In fact, this is your assignment today (and every day from here on out).

APPLICATION FOR TODAY

Find at least one person to help today, and help them to the best of your ability. It doesn't matter who they are and it's probably better if they are unlikely to ever use your services. It doesn't matter how efficient you are, or how well you match your abilities to how you help them. Just help them.

And don't forget to have a little fun.

EVERYONE WANTS TO HELP THE PRESIDENT

A while back, the president of a major nonprofit in the Seattle area invited someone I know, we'll call him Buck, to join him at his office for a meeting with a few others. Buck didn't know what the meeting was for. He really didn't even read his invitation, but he changed his calendar to make the meeting and showed up extra early.

Buck pulled up to the historic building the nonprofit is based in, checked in with the receptionist and was escorted to the president's enormous office. The room was lined with dark wood, floor to ceiling paneled windows and bookshelves on all sides. More than a dozen others had arrived even earlier than Buck and were gathered around a large conference table. When the host arrived, he opened the conversation by telling everybody that someone once told him, "As president, you have the power to convene." And he was right. Over a dozen people showed up for this meeting and I wonder how many of them came, like Buck, without even knowing what it was about.

The fact is, everyone wants to help the president. If the President of the United States invited you to join him at the White House for a meeting, would you make it a priority? I don't care who you voted for, almost anyone would dip into their savings or get a new credit card to book that flight. That's the power of being the President, or any president.

Power attracts lots of people

who want to help.

The problem is, most of us don't have the president of a regional nonprofit, much less the President of the United States, inviting us to his house for advice. We certainly can't just sit around waiting for that phone call. We have to start helping the people around us and we have to start now. That will probably mean helping people who are far from the top of the ladder, but that's fine. There's actually incredible power in helping those at the bottom, even if we're on the same rung as they are. Remember how helping isn't about us, it's about helping? If we truly believe that, we don't need to wait until someone important ask us for help. In fact, to a person with a pure helper spirit, everyone is important. Word spreads about such helpful people and it doesn't take long for their reputation to begin to precede them. Over time, if you focus on helping the people already in your life, you'll find that your circle expands, both outward and upward. It may be that thirty years down the road, after building a reputation of helping others no matter who they are, you'll find you're in the same enviable position as this nonprofit president. You'll have the power to convene and others, even influential others, might just rearrange their schedules to meet with you. And it will have all started because you were willing to help the people around you.

APPLICATION FOR TODAY

Think about a person who has helped you in your life and received little to nothing in return. Write a handwritten thank you note to that person and put it in the mail.

HELP PEOPLE. GET OFF STAGE.

I love the scene from *That Thing You Do* when Tom Hanks is talking to the band about their first big performance at a fair. One of the band asks, "What if they want an encore?" Tom replies, "You unplug and you run. Run off stage."

Scarcity creates demand. Even helpful people can overstay their welcome and everyone wants an encore. Everyone wants praise for what they've done, especially when what they've done is barely praiseworthy. Everyone is fishing for a compliment. Everyone hopes if they hang around long enough you'll eventually give them a little something to get lost. So when you make yourself scarce you separate yourself from all those other self-promoters. You prove how self-confident and self-actualized you are. We see this everywhere. When someone doesn't need you, they become more desirable. It's a little like playing hard to get—and everyone loves that guy/girl who doesn't need you.

Just imagine being in the shoes of that influential person who is used to everyone in the world coming up to them with their hand out, used to every compliment being another suck up attempt, every relationship turning into a one way pork fest. Now imagine someone approaches Miss Influential, solves a huge problem she's been grappling with, then disappears. How unique does that person suddenly become? You can bet they're going to be remembered. Especially if he appears again, just when Miss Influential needs his help, and is gone just as quickly. Soon, Miss Influential will be searching the internet, looking for our hero. How would you like to have influential people searching for you? That's the difference between helpeters and marketers. People search for helpeters like Lois Lane searched for Superman. Spammers, on the other hand, are mostly a pain in the ass. No one's riffling through their jacket pockets for the business card of that one salesperson who wouldn't leave them alone at a cocktail party.

Help someone, then disappear before you wear out your welcome. Don't worry, people tend to

remember helpful people.

APPLICATION FOR TODAY

Help someone today and then walk away. This could be as simple as pulling out a chair for a stranger at your favorite lunch spot on your way out the door. You could give someone you know a call with a tip or connection and then excuse yourself pleasantly, but quickly, from the conversation. Another idea is to meet with someone for 30 minutes and talk only about them and how you can help them, then make sure you run out of time before you get a chance to talk about how they can help you. When they apologize for talking about themselves the entire time let them know you'd much rather learn about them than talk about yourself anyway. And mean it! This isn't some smarmy manipulation, it's a shift in how you see and approach the world.

HELPING YOUR TARGET MARKET

At a certain point in any helpeter's journey, they have to become efficient in who they help. There is great reward for helping people who cannot help you in return, and you should never lose the desire to help such people. As you strive to be as helpful as possible, though, you'll find that doing so can actually impact your sales without violating the purity of your intentions. Getting a return on your investment is a very good thing and it's actually a natural byproduct of being more helpful and less self-focused. There are three main stages in the journey to being an effective helpeter.

STAGE ONE

First, if you're helping someone who is behind you in their career path, someone who is downstream from you or who can't return the favor in any way, you should expect them to take part in the process. You should expect them to do something with the help you give them. So if you give them homework assignments and they don't do the homework, or you make connections and they don't follow-up, stop helping them. The reality is, you can't help someone who won't help themselves and if you persist you're no longer being helpful. You're enabling and that's not only unhelpful, it's damaging. There are times when persisting with someone you care about deeply is a beautiful thing but in most situations, if you're volunteering your time and money to help someone, you should expect that they honor your investment by taking your advice seriously and making an effort to implement it. If they do not make an effort, you're not just wasting your time, you're wasting theirs. In this case you would be more helpful by telling them you can no longer meet with them. It's up to you how direct you are. Some people might benefit from you telling them bluntly why you won't meet with them. With other people it may be better to make a pleasant excuse and let the relationship fall away.

Some people, before they'll even set up an appointment, require an agreement that the person they're meeting with will implement their advice. You can really only do this if you're in high demand. Keep in mind that your requirement that they implement your advice isn't about not wasting your time. It's about not wasting theirs because helping is others-centered. Even if you get discouraged by people who don't want to make the effort to take your advice, be very careful to never lose the desire to help those downstream from you.

STAGE TWO

A second way to increase the impact of your helping is to be selective about helping people who are primarily upstream from you. They're ahead of you in their careers, they have more influence, they have more experience and wisdom to share or they have the ability to buy your service or product. Everyone needs someone upstream helping them along, but the moment you focus exclusively on helping those who are ahead of you is the moment you prove you're really only concerned with helping yourself.

Keep helping people downstream from you, but be prudent about who you help. You can, after all, only help a finite number of people. You might as well help those you can help most effectively. When you match your effectiveness to the people you help, you'll find that you're more likely to reach your goals, even if it's in a roundabout way.

Let's look at a practical example of how stage two might play out. If you're a manager at an F500 company, you would do well to find ways to help those 1-3 levels above you in the chain of command at your company and at similar companies that you might want to work for someday. Not only can these people help mentor you up your career path, they can offer valuable insights into how to perform in your current position, making you more valuable to your employer.

STAGE THREE

The third stage, and the pinnacle of helpeting effectiveness, is really an extension of stage two. This stage requires that you know exactly who has the highest probability of helping you reach your goals and that you focus with laser intensity on this target market. These do not have to be the exact people who would buy your services. They could be a referral partner who has the ability to send you dozens of new clients every year. If it is a customer you target, it shouldn't be just any customer. It should be your perfect customer. Someone you'd enjoy working with, someone with the money and desire to buy your product or service and someone who is likely to connect you to other customers like them.

Stage three is exemplified in the following situation. If you own a sign company, you would do well to find ways to serve commercial property managers. These property managers constantly have new small businesses come into their buildings, small businesses that need a lot of new signs to get up and running. By focusing on helping these property managers, or other potential high volume referral sources, you're greatly increasing the reach of your helpeting. For each person you help in this category, you're getting exponentially more in return.

It's important to note that focusing your helpfulness isn't just good for you. If it was, it wouldn't be in line with helpeting's primary principle of always being others-centered. Targeting certain people to help is better for them, too. When you're focused in who you help, you can become better at how you help. As we'll discuss later, how you help your target audience should also be more in line with your specific talents so you're offering more value. This focus allows you to cut out all the extraneous noise that might detract from your ability to help others to the best of your ability.

APPLICATION FOR TODAY

Identify the stage you are at currently in your journey toward becoming famously helpful. How can you move to the next stage or, if you are in stage three, how can you better target your helpeting on those high quality referral sources? Write a list of people you can help in the stage you are currently in and in the stages above you. Write down at least one way you can help each of these people, and then do it.

MAKE TIME TO HELP THOSE WHO CAN'T REPAY YOU

So we know from the last chapter that smart helpeters learn to focus their energy on helping people who can lead to a higher likelihood of increasing sales for their company. But you must walk a fine line between being efficient with your investment and making helping all about you. If you cross that line, your sales results will diminish. You must always make time to help those who can't help you back, those who have little to no chance of giving you anything in return. We're not talking karma here or a belief that the universe is kind to the generous. Though I do believe there is a God who repays those who serve the least among us, you don't even have to believe that to see why it's important to help those who can't help you in return. If you only help those who can help you, you're really helping people to help yourself. If this is your approach, you're not helping so much as making cold, calculated investments in order to get something for yourself. This, if taken further, leads to manipulation, self-serving, selfishness, demanding repayment, anger when you don't get something in return for your investment, etc. Smart people, especially influential ones, will see through you eventually and you'll end up seeing your results drop.

One of the issues that complicates this philosophy is the fact that some of the most self-centered, unhelpful, arrogant people in the world are also some of the most successful. How can helpeting be a true principle worth applying in your company if that's true? Because you're not one of those people. If you were, I don't think you'd be reading this book. Some people can get ahead in life by sheer force of talent, personality, charisma, intelligence, connections, inheritance or last name. I believe these people would do better if they applied the principles of helpeting, too, but they don't have to in order to be successful because the balance of luck is tipped in their favor. Most people don't have such fortunate circumstances from which to launch their business or career. You may not possess once-in-a-generation creative talent. You may not be able to get the job as CEO of the 49ers because your parents own the team. But you can rise far above your peers and even achieve greater success than those at the top of the top if you apply helpeting.

That's not a promise, because I can't guarantee your success. Why? Because everyone has limitations and there are a lot of things that factor into your success besides your marketing. All I can guarantee is that helpeting will take you further than any other marketing practice I've discovered. I do guarantee that you can have more fun doing it and that you can sleep better at night by focusing on helping others rather than tooting your own horn. How can I guarantee that? Not only have I experienced it firsthand and seen it at work in successful, happy, fulfilled people around me, but you can see it in the most helpful, honest book of all time: the Bible. Now you might disagree with a lot of what's in the Bible, but if you take the time to study what it has to say about practical wisdom for living, you might find there's a lot of good insight in those pages. In Mark 10:24 Jesus tells his followers, who have just asked how to become great, that if anyone wants to become great, they must become the servant of all. Greatness, according to Jesus, is serving.

We buy the books of the people who help us with their content. We're giving those people our attention and, in a sense, placing them into a teacher/mentor role over us by listening to what they say. If they cease to be helpful and start trying to sell us their next workshop, we can remove them from their position over us. Now if millions of people place one person over them because of how helpful that person is, it's easy to argue that this person is great. What better measurement of greatness is there than to have millions of people listening to your words and taking your advice?

Helping is about the people you're helping. This principle plays out it so many ways. For example, one of the best bits of insight I've ever received about public speaking is that it's all about the audience. As soon as a speaker forgets that, they lose. Nobody wants to hear someone speak purely for the sake of hearing that person speak. They listen because they believe that what they hear will be helpful. This is true even with the most famous people. It's just that famous people are well-known for helping a lot of people in a certain way. Maybe they're a comedian and they help people by making them smile. Or they're a famous author and they help people with their intelligent, applicable ideas. Or they're a motivational speaker and they help people by offering inspiration. It doesn't matter how famous you are, people don't care about you so much as they care about how you can help them. So when a speaker steps onto the stage, sees all those faces staring back, hears the applause and the audience laughing at his jokes, he has a choice. He can believe all these people are here for his sake. This will, however, lead to him losing his audience. Why? The speaker is helping himself.

No one has time to bother

with another person who is only interested in helping themselves.

The other option for this speaker is to focus on his audience. Instead of helping himself by telling stories about his own greatness or hawking his new book or selling a web series, if this speaker gives practical insights with humor and engages his audience, the people listening will want more. They'll seek out his books because he was helpful. They'll want to buy his web series or attend his next event without the sales pitch. This is helpeting at work.

Just like a speaker must make their talk about the audience, helpeters don't ever lose sight of the need to help people upstream and down. They realize helping isn't about them, it's about others. It's impossible to focus only on helping upstream people without make helping all about you. This is the reason that, whether you believe in karma or just want a maximum return on investment, you have to make space for helping people who can't help you. It's a way to make sure your helping motives are pure. And as a bonus, it's not unheard of for that person, the one you thought could never repay you, to end up leading to some great business opportunity. You never know who that person across from you is connected to or who they'll become in the future. They might be the CEO of your next huge client relationship and they'll remember how you helped them without expecting anything in return.

APPLICATION FOR TODAY

Set aside a certain amount of time each week or each month to help those who are unlikely to give you anything in return. This could be volunteering at a soup kitchen, serving in you church's Sunday school class, teaching at a community college or connecting fresh graduates to great networkers you know. Put the time on your calendar and guard it carefully. This could be one of the most important parts of your week.

HOW YOU HELP MATTERS

The first time I met Ron Kranz, we sat 20 feet apart in the 520 Bar and Grill for twenty minutes, both wondering when the other guy was going to show up. I was busy on my phone trying to find a picture of Ron on LinkedIn, starting to feel the silly need to remind my waitress that I was still waiting for someone, when I spotted him across the restaurant. We spent the next two hours talking about business and how Ron could help me with the coaching services he offers. Before we left, Ron gave me a small spiral-bound book emblazoned with his company name. He gave me a few other things too, tools he uses to help his clients clarify their direction and achieve their business goals. One was a custom to-do list, another was a pad of paper with the words "What I'm not going to do today" on each page.

I flipped through the book later that night as I sat on the couch, some made for TV remake playing in the background. The pages in Ron's book were thick and bright and well designed. I found myself starting to do a few of the exercises he recommended and before I knew it I was over halfway through the book. The things Ron talked about, the system he uses to help small businesses define and achieve their goals, were reinforced in the little book and I felt a connection to Ron. I also saw his expertise, his attention to detail and excellence, and I felt that he was successful, at least successful enough to pay someone to print and design that book for him. Plus, Ron was generous with me. He gave me something that had cost him time and effort and that contained some of his most valuable intellectual property. Ron helped me, but more importantly for Ron, he helped me in a way that established himself as an expert in his field. He helped me in a way that allowed me to sample his services. And I wanted more. I wanted to hire Ron to help me with my business.

When you're first starting in helpeting, it's okay to help people in any way you can. Help them with their laundry. Help them find a date for Friday night. Help them with their homework. Help them with their home remodel. Helping people is always good. It's just that there's a way to make your helping *more* good. That's what Ron did. This kind of helping is not just more good for you, it's more good for your target market. It's important to remember that anything that's purely better for you erodes the principles of helpeting, which is always others-centered. Focusing instead on how you help people around you in your strongest areas of talent allows you to increase the degree to which you help people. For example, if you're a dentist you may be able to offer a helping hand by offering to patch up clothes for your neighbors, but you'd be a lot more valuable if you offered to fill your neighbor's cavities.

There's a flip side, though. Just as you should always make space for helping people who can't help you, you should also make space for helping in ways that don't align with your strongest skill set. I think this is necessary in order to remind ourselves that we're not nearly as big a deal as we often think we are. If we're always uppity about only doing the things we do best, we're like the salesman who won't do the dishes or the actor who won't carry groceries in from the car. Sometimes we should just do what needs to be done, even if we're not great at it. As long as we're making room for doing things we're not great at, simply as a way of helping out when help is needed, it's a good idea to be efficient with our helping. In other words, we can and should align the way we help people with our greatest talents. Along those lines, we should help people with activities that pay us the greatest hourly wage or bring us the most joy. For example, if you, because of your experience, connections and talents, are worth $50 an hour as a copywriter and $100 an hour as a website designer, it would be more efficient to help people with web design, advice on SEO or articles about how to make money online. Helping people in this way will highlight your skills as a web designer and will in turn help you get more of that kind of work, which pays you more and allows you to either provide more for your family or spend less time working. Balance into that equation what you enjoy doing most. You might make more money repairing computers, but maybe you enjoy decorating cakes more than fixing PCs. Only you know what you need to earn for a living and what you enjoy most. It could be that you do one thing for income and another in your free time. You should be able to find ways to help people using both of those skill sets so you can set yourself up to earn more money and enjoy life at the same time.

APPLICATION FOR TODAY

Write down the thing you do that earns the most money. If you're a nonprofit, this could be the activity that generates the most financial support. If you're a business, this could be your most profitable product or service line. If you're an individual, this could be a combination of your greatest talent and the talent that generates the most value for an employer. In addition to this, write down the thing you enjoy most. For a company, this could be the product or service you're most excited about for the future. For a nonprofit, this could be the work you enjoy most as an organization or the work with the greatest impact. Hopefully these two items align and your most profitable activity is also your favorite. If they don't, is there a way to change what you're doing to make them align? If not, keep them separate and start to brainstorm ways you can help people that aligns with these activities. In the next section, we'll discuss a number of examples that might help you generate some ideas.

UNLIMITED WAYS TO HELP

Tully's Coffee on Main Street in Bellevue, Washington is widely known as *the* place to go to network. It's always hard to find a table, everyone appears to be some sort of mover or shaker in the community and everyone is networking all the time. A lot of business gets done in that little coffee shop. If Tully's on Main, as it's known around the region, is the king of Seattle area networking, Jeff Rogers is the king of Tully's on Main. It's actually hard to have a meeting with Jeff there because you'll be interrupted about every five minutes as someone new walks in and briefly catches up with him.

Jeff is quick to smile, kindhearted and genuinely cares about everyone he meets. He's about the best entry point to networking I can think of. What I mean by that is if you're new to town and need to get your network running quickly, no one will help you more than Jeff. When I was first getting my marketing agency off the ground, Jeff helped me tremendously by hiring my firm to produce some videos for his consulting agency, OneAccord. While producing these videos, I had the opportunity to learn a lot about Jeff's approach to sales. Not surprisingly, Jeff is a major helpeter. When he meets with new contacts he has a couple of rules. First, no business. He doesn't want to talk shop. He uses his first meeting to really get to know someone. They talk about things like family, the Seahawks (or Mariners if you're a suffering Seattle baseball fan) and travel. The whole time they're talking, Jeff's mind is churning. He's looking for ways to help the person across from him and the primary way he does this is by making connections. Jeff will introduce you to people he thinks would be a good fit or to someone who can help you along on your journey.

Jeff teaches a sales system that involves setting three meetings each workday at the same spot. He advises his friends to pick a central coffee shop and show up there from 8 to 11 every morning. At the end of each day's meetings, he suggests they then open up their computer and provide three introductions to each of the people they met with that day. Jeff is living out a principle much discussed in academic research known as structural holes. Structural holes are connections between networks that aren't otherwise connected. If you have a relationship with someone who is part of a completely different circle of people than your own and very few people in your respective circles know each other, you're more valuable to everyone in your network because you have the power to bridge these two groups. Jeff is this sort of person. He helps people by connecting them to helpful people they don't yet know. This is one of the most popular ways networkers help each other, but there are many others. In the back of a book called *Network Like A Pro*, Ivan Misner, the founder of worldwide networking system BNI, provides a score card for determining whether you'll be successful in networking. On the card are examples of networking actions, such as helping someone get a speaking gig or providing a referral. The whole system basically boils down to the idea that the more you help people, the more successful you will be. Ivan is preaching the power of helpeting.

There are no limits to how you can help people.

I've seen people find numerous ways to put their expertise to work helping others. Here are just a few examples of what I've seen that you could do today:

- Write an ebook that gives away your very best ideas, so that when people see your system they want to hire you to implement it for them.

- Blog on the same topic as above--then turn your posts into an ebook when you have enough content.

- Provide a free sample of your work, such as an audit, or offer to work for a month at no charge.

- Make connections to referral partners or customers.

- Speak on your topic of knowledge.

- Host online webinars, podcasts or forums on topics that are helpful to your customers.

- Buy copies of your favorite books and carry them with you to hand out to people you meet who would benefit.

- Create a series of videos that train your customers in your area of expertise.

- Do in-depth comparisons between services that compliment what you offer.

- Compile a treasure chest of resources that would benefit your customers. This is doubled up help, actually, because you'll also be helping the creators of these resources by giving them more exposure.

- Comment on other people's blogs/social media pages. This helps keep their pages active and they will take notice.

- Promote helpful services in your email list. Just don't do it in a spammy way. You might want to explain in your email that you're getting nothing out of promoting these services and that you believe your audience would benefit by knowing about them.

- Help people get speaking gigs or otherwise build their platform. You can feature guests on your blog and on your social media pages.

- Create a list of the best service providers in a number of areas pertinent to your target market. Take the time to format it well so you can easily give it away to people you meet.

- Sponsor a personality/aptitude test and allow your target market to take the test for free at your expense.

- Buy articles from *Harvard Business Review* or other high quality sources and email them to your target market. Just make sure you have the rights to do so—you might need to buy a license for each person you email.

- Consult with a client for free, meet with their board of directors and do a private presentation that doesn't include a sales pitch. Just genuinely try to help.

These are just a few possible ways that you can help your target market. Only you know what they need and what you have to offer. Find a way to match those two up in a free, premium offering that establishes you as not only helpful, but an expert in your field. Every one of these methods is your first entry point with any potential customer. If you do a shabby job with helping people, your customers will assume you'll do a shabby job with everything. This is not the time to skimp. You must spend the time and money to make your help excellent. The world is full of people trying to help others for their own gain and the world is therefore full of crappy help.

The best way for you to stand out is to have excellent

help, help so amazing that it shocks your customers to know you'd give it away.

I sat next to a financial advisor on a flight one time who would fly to meet a potential client anywhere in the country and then meet with that person several times over the course of more than a year without getting a single penny. I later found out that this advisor is one of the most successful in the country. His approach truly embodies the essence of helpeting and I'm certain it plays a major role in his success.

APPLICATION FOR TODAY

Write down a list of the ways you might be able to help people. Take an inventory of your relationships then come up with some ideas for how to align your skills with a resource that you can offer. Start to compile these helpful tools and be ready to offer them to others when the opportunity arises.

THE
UNHELPFUL
QUESTION

You're having coffee with your perfect prospect. The conversation has been going well. You're eager to help them and, full disclosure, even more eager to get on their good side so you have a better shot at getting their business. You've given them the floor and encouraged them to talk about themselves. Suddenly, you realize that while they've been talking, you've been daydreaming about doing business together. The conversation is wrapping up and, since you're committed to helpeting, you say, "It's been really great getting to know you. How can I help you?" If you've been in a situation like this before, on either side of the table, you can probably guess what the other person says. Usually something like, "Well, thanks for the offer. I can't really think of anything right now." Then the person offering to help responds, "If anything comes to mind, I'm an email away."

Anybody who takes this approach will be frustrated with helpeting. They might feel like they're not getting any results from their coffee meetings. They might even find the people they meet with less likely to want to meet again. Why is that? What went wrong? They were only trying to help, after all. The problem with asking, "How can I help you?" is that it's not helpful. You're actually putting a burden on the person you wanted to help by leaving it to them to figure out what you can do for them. That's like being hired to create a logo for someone and then asking them to send you three or four logos they've created that they like so you know what direction to take.

A true helpeter doesn't ask

how they can help.

They take the burden of figuring out how to help all on their own. Being truly helpful requires listening intently and being so present in a conversation that you're able to make the connection between what you have to offer and what the person sitting across from you needs. During a conversation, you must be constantly searching for opportunities to help, looking for clues the indicate the other person's need and then making the connection between their need and what you have to offer. When you make those connections, resist the urge to blurt them out. Instead, jot them down and keep listening. Sometimes when you're meeting with someone, it's going to be really obvious how you can help. If you're a CFO consultant and someone is meeting with you because they asked a friend for a connection to a good CFO, how you can help is abundantly obvious. If you ask, "How can I help you?" you're being passive when you could be in charge and proactive. Devise an easy way to showcase your expertise and help them with whatever CFO needs come up during the conversation. Don't offer to do a proposal. Instead, proceed as if you already have the business. Set up an appointment to meet with their team or ask for access to their financials so you can give them some insight into their issues. The particulars of how you offer to help are dependent on the level of trust you feel with this person, the content of your conversation and a million other things. But you'll have a lot more success if you come up with your best idea on how to help them rather than depending on them to sort it all out.

Part of the problem with expecting others to tell you how you can help them is that they don't know you very well. They certainly don't know all the people in your circle, nor do they have the time to research your skills, background and experience. People are looking for others to take control of a situation and run with it. They're already trying to sort out a million things—figuring out how you can help doesn't need to be one of them. A self-confident expert who has an idea of where to take the relationship and understands the benefits to both sides is a breath of fresh air. Someone who sets up meetings for the sake of meeting is just the opposite.

In fact, nothing is more frustrating than endlessly meeting while nothing is actually accomplished. No one has time for that. That person sitting across from you is meeting you for a reason. Maybe you were referred to them blindly. Maybe they need something that you provide. Maybe they're interviewing you for a contract or job. Whatever the reason, show them how different you are from 99% of the rest of the world by taking action and making your own suggestions for how to move forward, illustrating your commitment to making the relationship beneficial for them. There are some very practical ways to do this. An easy method is to go into the meeting armed with a notepad that says, "Ways I will help this person" across the top. I usually use my phone to create an email to myself with the subject, "To-do list from my meeting with ___." Then, when an idea strikes during the meeting I take out my phone, type a short line that will jog my memory later, and keep listening. Keeping these notes short is vital—nothing says you don't care about the person across from you more than staring at your phone while they're talking. If the ideas you come up with aren't immediate needs, save some of them in a CRM (customer relationship management) database for later. You're going to need these ideas to help this person in the future so you can continue building the relationship. Plus, it's too much to bombard them all at once with every resource, connection and offer you can think of. Far better to spread it out over the course of six months so they know you're still thinking of them.

APPLICATION FOR TODAY

Before you go into your next meeting, create an email to yourself or a note on your Moleskine titled "How I'm going to help this person." Then during your conversation take notes on ideas for how to help the person you're meeting with. After the meeting, as soon as possible and definitely no later than that evening, take action on those items. Help in one or two concrete ways immediately in your follow-up thank you email. Then keep notes on ways you'll be able to help them in the future. I've found that emailing or calling once a month with a new way to help is the best cycle for staying top of mind without being overly assertive.

FROM MARKETING TO NETWORKING

A lot of people misunderstand networking. Both those who avoid it and those who engage in it tend to think that networking is the domain of slick hair, cocktail parties, superficial conversation and stacks of business cards. But good networking is built on the principles of helpeting. It's about having relationships with people for the mutual benefit of both individuals. So the guy who keeps looking over your shoulder in search of someone more important to talk to, or whose focus is on handing out a record number of business cards at a fundraiser, is not going to reap much from his effort.

Good networkers understand that they must be helpful to people in order to build a relationship with them.

You don't have to have strong relationships with everyone in your network for your network to be effective. In fact, it's a good idea to have a large number of people in your network you don't meet with very often but still share a degree of trust and respect with. This gives you a large amount of reach because of the variety of relationships. Just be careful to not confuse a connection on LinkedIn with someone in your network. If they don't know you, and if they don't have a degree of trust with you, they're not a part of your actual network. It's easy to lose track of people you don't see often, but one of the coolest things about helpeting is that it's like networking on steroids. There's a limit to the number of people you or I can meet with in a year, but helpeting makes it possible for you to build relationships with thousands or even millions of people. This is where the difference between it's who you know versus it's who knows you comes into the equation. If it's all who you know, you're limited by the number of people you can keep track of. If it's about who knows you, you can scale your ability to serve millions.

Authors like Seth Godin have done a great job of this. Seth's built a huge tribe of people who are willing to help him launch his next book and spread the word about his latest endeavors because he's been helpful through his content to this tribe for years. Does Seth know everyone he helps? Not a chance. But everyone in Seth's tribe knows Seth. He's opened himself up to being known and has built trust through his consistent quality and the volume of his content. People like Seth are everywhere, building trust with an audience so vast that people thousands of miles away, people they've never actually met, feel deeply connected to and concerned about them. That's the power of helpeting. It scales your networking to a level you could never achieve if you had to know each of the people who know you.

APPLICATION FOR TODAY

Think of a few ways that you can help people without meeting with them one-on-one. How can you scale your ability to help your target market? Make a plan to start doing more of these things, diverting a little time from your one-on-one activities.

GETTING CREDIT

Helpeters must walk a line between ensuring they get credit for helping people and helping people for the right reasons regardless of who gets the credit. If you help a thousand people anonymously, you may be living out the principles of helpeting but it won't help you directly increase in your sales. On the other hand, if you insist on getting credit for everything that you do, you run the risk of making helping all about you. It seems fitting to close this section on becoming known by helping people by pointing out that it's okay to get props for what you've done. It's about becoming *famously* helpful, after all. Just be sure to hold your desire for attention with a loose grip and allow credit to come on its own. You don't need to force it. People will notice what you do and they will talk about you behind your back, in the best possible sense. You may not get credit for every way you help people, and I don't think you should try to, but helpful people can't be hidden. They're too in demand. The more helpful someone becomes, the more famous they become for it. This is natural and shouldn't be something to avoid or be ashamed of. Just don't let it go to your head. Keep helping and allow the credit to come when it does.

PART 2. INCREASE TRUST THROUGH CONSISTENCY OVER TIME

CONTENT MARKETING

For the last decade at least, savvy marketers have been applying the principles of helpeting under the banner of content marketing. Properly executed, this is really just one facet of helpeting. Content marketing, in simple terms, uses blogging, ebooks, white papers and social media to provide content to an audience. Usually, this content is available in exchange for a small price, such as a like on Facebook or an email address. Over time, the content marketer is hoping to build a more complete profile of their audience by asking for more information each time they initiate a download. This allows them to qualify leads and move them through the sales funnel toward a closed deal. This is a prime example of what helpeting looks like in the real world and it comes with the dangers any helpeter faces. Content marketing, like any form of helpeting, can become too self-promotional or hype-based. This can boost results short term, but it ends up creating a list of leads who are more interested in chasing the next shortcut and will often leave relatively quickly. However, if content marketing is based on helping people with superior content that fosters personal and professional growth, if it's well done and doesn't come off as obnoxious or self-focused, it can be a perfect tool for helping your target audience and becoming famously helpful.

One powerful tenant of content marketing is transitioning your audience from being casual consumers of your ideas to thinking of you as a thought leader in your space. It's a slow process that starts with someone begrudgingly giving you their email address in exchange for an ebook or some similar offer. If you're lucky, they won't unsubscribe with the first email. Over the next few months your emails will probably go straight to spam or get buried under the hundred other emails that came in over the weekend. Then one day, this person might stumble upon one of your emails with a subject line that speaks directly to a problem they're facing at that exact moment. There's a good chance they'll sit down, click the link to your blog and read the post. Or at least skim it. Hopefully you spent the time and effort to make this post helpful and you deliver on the promise your headline made, because this might be the only chance you'll ever have to convince this person to engage with you again. If you hold up your end of the silent agreement, they'll begin to read your emails with more frequency and, eventually, something magical will happen. When this person is confronted with a problem, they'll actually open up their internet browser, type in your URL and search your website for answers. This is the moment you become a thought leader to this person. How much easier do you think it will be to sell your product or service to this person now that they see you as a thought leader? I bet you could get coffee with this person if you wanted to, whereas six month earlier they wouldn't even click on your email. Behold, the power of content marketing.

The other cool thing about being helpful, whether you're meeting with someone in person or sharing your ideas on a blog, is that:

People evaluate you

differently when you're trying to help them instead of get into their pocketbook.

What's the first thing you do when a salesperson calls or walks up to you on a car lot? Your shoulders raise, you try to look invisible, you shout out while they're still fifty feet away, "I'm just looking." A salesperson is automatically in a subservient position to the person they are trying to sell to. One person is the boss, the other is the salesperson. If you can manage to set up a situation where you interact with a customer as their equal, or even better, as their advisor, so much the better. Instead of being the salesman, you're a trusted source. You're on equal footing and your opinion matters. Your time matters. Imagine that. Of course, this is a principle you're already familiar with. Who are you more likely to take a product recommendation from—a mentor or a salesperson?

How can you level the playing field with your next employer, customer or donor? Part of this starts with your own mindset. How do you see yourself? Are you equal to your target market or are you desperate for their attention? Once you've established a healthy mindset, focus on delivering value rather than getting something for yourself, and you'll be well on your way.

APPLICATION FOR TODAY

Before you go into your next meeting with a prospect, spend five minutes reminding yourself of the value you bring to the relationship. Then conduct the meeting as an equal, not a salesperson desperate for attention. Helpeters have much to offer, and they know it.

SLOW AND STEADY

If there's one thing that separates helpful people from successful helpful people it's consistency. Anyone can be helpful once, even if only by accident, but it takes a special person to be helpful again and again over a long period of time.

People are wary by nature. It starts in grade school and continues through all of life. They've been double-crossed too many times and eventually learn not to trust anybody they've just met. It's not that they're unwilling to trust others. Most of the people I know, even the most influential, are looking for people to trust, they just want to be sure. How can you make someone sure of you? Consistency. People want to know you're dependable. Even if you're a total screw up, it's comforting to be the predictable screw up. They know you're always going to show up 15 minutes late and they can either decide to deal with that or severe the relationship. It's the people who show up on time mostly but forget about appointments 20% of the time that people have a real problem trusting. They just never know what they're going to get.

The world is constantly changing. This puts enormous strain on our minds as we try to cope with everything going on around us. We, as humans, are desperate for something steady.

We want to know someone's going to be there for us

when we need them.

Great helpeters benefit greatly from this desire because they're more consistent than everyone around them. Consistency doesn't happen overnight, which is why one major factor in helpeting is patience. Playing the long game. I've found the more influential a person is, the more patience impresses them. They manage the large volume of requests coming at them by generally ignoring everything. The messages that get through come from established, trusted advisors. If you keep trying to be helpful and you're not upset when they deny you or don't respond, and if you persevere, trying again maybe six months later and again six months after that, all the while growing in your ability to help others, this highly influential person will see it. Even if you only get a millimeter of their attention, they will slowly realize that you're not like all the other piranhas who are constantly trying to get a piece of them. Many of them will eventually let you in.

Stage two of helpeting is all about making it easy for people to think of you as consistent, and patience is a huge part of that. In fact, the most important effect of consistency and patience with helpeting is that it enables you to be top of mind over a long period of time for your target market. People don't buy something the first time their hear about it, nor do they buy from someone the first time they meet them. This is for a variety of reasons besides the simple matter that it takes time to make good decisions. If you can work on building trust with this person over time, you'll be there when they're ready. By that time, you'll have built up a storehouse of trust with them, making it even easier for them to sign a deal with you quickly.

Perhaps the best part is that once you've built trust with someone and become their advisor, you have no competition. Successful people don't become successful by second guessing a team member who is performing for them. Successful people find people they work well with and then go to them again and again. You see this in movies all the time. It's why the same directors and actors seem to team up on so many projects. That director has found that they like working with this person and they get the performance they need. Once you've found that person, you stop looking for someone new. The same is true for helpeting. Once you've become a trusted advisor to your perfect prospect, the chances are greatly diminished that they'll even get another bid or open up their search to a bigger pool of prospects. Why bother when they already have you?

Great marketing, even helpeting, doesn't make the sale. It earns people's

trust. That's what this stage is all about.

THE IMPORTANCE OF PATIENCE

People quit far more often than they fail. The difference between failure and quitting is the difference between greatness and mediocrity. Great people fail. Mediocre people quit.

Helpeters don't quit helping people no matter how boring it gets, how shiny the new distractions are or what other opportunities present themselves. No matter how little thanks they receive, no matter how bad the press reviews are or how nasty the troll comments get or how slowly the follower counts grow or how many people unsubscribe or how many critics tell them they shouldn't quit their day job, helpeters keep going. The world is filled with people who are willing to try something for a while. This is why workout equipment is so cheap on Craigslist.

People know how to lose weight, but most don't have the drive, the commitment and the patience. The same is true for helpeting. The principles of becoming famously helpful are not new. They've been used by the most successful people on earth since the beginning of time. Yet most people don't achieve a great level of success from helping people because sooner or later they get tired of helping. This is the counterintuitive part about helping people. Helping is hard. It's way harder than selling. It's harder than working for minimum wage. It's harder than sitting on a couch. It's harder than hoarding our talents for ourselves. It might seem like helping would be easy because who wouldn't want to be helped? Part of the problem is there are so many people willing to "help" that you've got to cut through the clutter just to get someone's attention. Another part of the problem is that people are worried your help will actually create work or problems for them. Most of all, people are skeptical. They just assume you have an angle and they worry you're just trying to get close to them so they'll give you stuff.

People who become great through helping don't stop helping when it gets hard. They persist.

It takes time, but eventually people will see your true intentions, whether for good or bad. You can prove that you're different from all the other fake helpeters by playing the long game. You can increase your odds of success from helpeting by anticipating the ugly. Expect the troll comments and the one star reviews and the people who falsely report your emails as spam even though you can prove that they signed up, because helpeters aren't helping people in order to grow their mailing list or compile a portfolio of glowing reviews. They're helping because they want to help people and they know that it requires persistence to break down the barriers people put up all the time. Helpeters believe they can help people and that helping is worth sticking with it.

APPLICATION FOR TODAY

Identify some potential barriers that might cause you to quit helpeting. Maybe it's the budget it will require and your manager is going to demand immediate results or she'll pull the money. Maybe it's the fear of rejection by book reviewers. Whatever it is, write it down. Write out the worst possible case, then double it. If it takes twice as long, if you get twice as many negative reviews as positive reviews, if you're rejected by twice as many people as you thought possible, can you keep going? If you aspire to write an ebook to help people, go to one of your favorite books and read all the one star reviews. (If there are no one star reviews, that means the book hasn't been read by anyone. So you have to find a book that's popular enough to have at least ten.) Read those reviews and ask yourself, if these are the only sort I get, will I quit? Be honest with yourself. If the answer is yes, then you may not be ready to get started with helpeting, at least in that format.

THE SLOW STEADY CLIMB

Nothing is more beautiful than a slow, steady climb.

There are a few examples of people and companies who achieved great success or fame (not necessarily the same thing) in a short amount of time. Facebook. Walt Disney. Miley Cyrus. Because of magazines and the internet, we might start to think that this is the norm. That if we don't achieve immediate success our efforts are doomed to a long, miserable death. But the truth is that the vast majority of success comes over a long period of time. I think the slow and steady climb is the superior approach to life and business, and I base that belief on the testimony and observation of many successful people I've met with over the years. When you achieve huge success in a short time you're constantly in a place where you have to meet or exceed that success or people will be disappointed. Plus, it's easy to let success go to your head when you achieve a lot of it in a little time. You might start to read the press and believe what people are saying about you. The slow, steady climb, one in which you peak late, is ideal. You go out on top. You learn to appreciate what it takes to get to the top because you've worked so hard for so long. You're more generous with others, helping them achieve success, too, because you recognize the many people who helped you along the way. Besides, the odds are against the meteoric rise. While some people hit a home run in their first game, that's not a business plan. You can't set out to achieve that. If you do, you'll likely become one of the 99.9% of people who fail. This isn't to say that we should look down on those who have achieved a lot in a short time. Good for them! I just don't advise that you measure your results against the microscopic number of people who are featured on the cover of *Fast Company*. Shoot for stars, sure, you might reach them, but don't beat yourself up if you don't. Keep trying until you do, and keep the perspective that:

Most successful people throughout history reached the peak of their orbit late in life.

Helpeting is a way to help you achieve this long, steady rise. Most helpeter's audiences grow like a savings account. You plug a little money away, as much as you can afford, for a really long time and then you wake up one day to find you've got ten million bucks in the bank. The growth of helpeting's effect is painfully slow for a really long time until it hits some sort of critical mass and starts to accelerate. You start to run downhill. Everything becomes easier. People are no longer standing you up for your appointments. You have a lot more people requesting to meet with you rather than the other way around. People start showing up early to meet with you rather than strolling in ten minutes late.

That's not to say you can't expect any quick results. The cool part about helpeting is that you can see its effectiveness quite quickly. You're not likely to land on the moon in your first year, but helping people wields more power every time you try. As a practical guide, I've seen most people experience some measurable benefit from helpeting in the first year. They were able to get a better job. Their sales increased by 10%. They secured a new client or two. Small wins like that. Somewhere two to five years in, things really start to accelerate. Many people might be fine settling in at that rate of success, but others, those who keep pushing hard with helpeting for decades, are the ones who end up playing a big role in making this world a better place.

APPLICATION FOR TODAY

Who have you held up as a model for success? Do you need to adjust your expectation of what's likely and how long it might take? Do you find that those 30 under 30 lists depress you? Read a few biographies and company case studies that show a more realistic view of what it takes to make an impact. Don't give up on shooting as high as you want. Make big, if not at least somewhat realistic goals, and go for them. You should always aim high, just don't beat yourself up if or when you fall back to earth. Whenever you feel you're not measuring up to whatever preconceived notions of success you have, bring to mind the stories you uncover of those who won in long game.

THE AGGRESSIVE HELPER

You're excited about helping people. You have great ideas and are ready to push forward through any obstacle that dares to block your progress. A word of warning is due here: there is such a thing as too much.

Some people who genuinely want to help can go about it way too aggressively, which is a major put off to many people. Play it cool. If you have to, imagine someone you know, someone you look up to a lot, and imagine how they would handle your situation. Emulate them. How would they offer to help? How often would they follow-up with prospects? You can also be too persistent. Each person and situation is different and requires a different approach. Usually, the larger the discrepancy between your influence and theirs, the longer you should go between follow-ups. If you've found people who could become clients but don't have an immediate need, staying in touch once a month is a good frequency. If they have a more immediate need, then yes, once a week or more may be appropriate, depending on the situation. If the person is very influential and there's no immediate need, staying in touch twice a year is a good long-term strategy. Whatever you do, make these communications count. What I mean by that is be sure never to just check in with a potential client. Be helpful. Send them a resource, make a connection for them, nominate them to speak at an event — something in line with the themes of helpeting. You might even offer to do some free work for them or consult on an issue you know has come up in their organization. Do your research and know the opportunities that are available so you can be as specific as possible in your offer to help. If you've done your homework, and we'll talk more about this in the next section, they'll generally remember you and the fact that you'd like to do business with them. If you're not too intense in your communications, they're more likely to be open to the opportunity.

APPLICATION FOR TODAY

Look up the people you're trying to help in your personal network and make a note of who you will contact once a week, once a month or twice a year. You can create any time cycle that seems to fit based on your impression of the situation. Then set reminders using your calendar, a to-do list or any other means to get in touch with them in the appointed timeframe.

Plan out how you will help and be hands off with how you present your ideas. You don't constantly need to be talking about how you want to help. Just help as the need arises.

BLOGGING

One of the best ways to maintain awareness of your brand and build trust over time is with a blog. Blogs allow you to write about and establish your expertise in so many ways. Plus, when you create a content calendar, blogging can help you be consistent over time. A helpful, consistent blog is a dream tool for becoming famously helpful.

When it comes to communicating, today's world is far different than even just a decade ago. The public expects much of what they consume, even very high quality products, to be free. This is due in part to a few entrepreneurial organizations and thought leaders who realized they could give away their content and make money on the relatively small number of consumers who wished to go further. As more and more content creators caught on, consumers soon realized that they no longer needed to pay for these resources. Yet, despite the glut of content available today for free, blogging remains a great tool for reaching new people with our message, whether we're selling a product or inviting them to church. One reason blogging remains one of the best methods for reaching new consumers is simple — nothing better has emerged. The old ways of communicating, like advertising and direct or pushy sales, are still in use but have become almost completely ineffective. Today's consumers view these approaches as a turn off and will often immediately shut down when someone starts selling. In the noisy world we live in, it's nearly impossible for our tiny little message to break through the clutter, no matter how much we pay or how hard we try, but blogging can still be effective. Even with the enormous constraints on our target market's attention, if we blog better than our competitors do, we'll see results.

Blogging is a simple idea. You have something to sell, but instead of marketing it directly, you help your target market, usually with information that illustrates you as a content expert. The better and more helpful your content, the more highly your audience regards you. They become fans and return again and again to get resources from you, disregarding the countless others vying for their attention. They do this because you're consistently helpful. You don't waste their time. You don't take them for granted. You don't talk down to them. Maybe you even make them laugh a little. In short, you enrich their life. These fans aren't morons. They know what you do for a living. In fact, the more of your content they consume, the more they'll want to work with you. They may not initiate a transaction for months, but someday they will.

When the timing is right, the budget is set, the need becomes apparent, you'll be the

first person they think of.

Remember how success isn't about who you know, but about who knows you? And that the best way to be known by someone is to help them? If a stranger had the perfect solution to your biggest problem, a solution that was cheaper and easier than you had hoped possible, and they went out of their way to connect you to this solution, would you remember them? What if they did this for you three times over the course of six months? I bet they'd be on their way to being your first call when a problem came up. You can go from stranger to hero by simply helping. The bigger the problem you solve, the bigger the hero you become. And if you become a hero to the right people, you will always exceed your goals. Since blogging is ultimately about helping people, figure out who it is you want to know you and then get to know them really well. What do they need? What problems do they often face? How can you help them? Then get started. It's not a quick solution. Starting a blogging campaign today isn't going to help you meet your quota this month. But in the long run, there's no better method for building a business.

Once you start, you might be surprised at how much time this takes. Maybe too much time, a common issue many would be bloggers discover after they launch their blog. This is why the web is littered with sites where the last post is dated three years ago. These sites look stale. In fact, they look dead. Blogging is a lot of work and not everyone in your company is necessarily a good candidate to write for you. Before you start your blog, decide how many posts you want to do per month and create a backlog. That way, if things get busy you aren't scrambling to create something at the last minute. I've found in most situations that releasing a new blog once a week is best, but the ideal frequency can range from daily to once a month in most circumstances. Most blogs have several writers so the burden's not all on one person. You can also hire a freelancer or firm to do your blogging for you. Ghost writers can take a lot of the pressure of producing content off your shoulders, and it's easier than people think. Usually you do an interview over the phone and the writer creates a draft of your ideas. Good ghost writers will try to emulate your voice and make it sound like you wrote it. If you're expecting your employees to contribute to your blog you should consider investing in a ghost writer to clean up their posts, or at least a content editor to help them develop their ideas in a way that will stand up in comparison to the vast amount of high quality content available on the web for free. Remember that because so much content is available today, the best way to stand out and be successful is to create better content than the competition. This may sound daunting until you realize most people and companies don't take blogging seriously. They churn out stuff at the last minute that's full of cliches and tired ideas. If you want to beat these people, you can, but you have to be committed to a higher level of quality. Realistically this is going to require a full-time writer or editor, either someone on your staff or an outside freelancer or agency. Occasionally, there are individuals and companies that have the talent in house already, but I've found that this is rare.

The most counter-

intuitive principle in blogging is that you gain people who want to pay for your help by giving away your best ideas.

It's easy to spot someone who isn't likely to succeed in blogging because they hold their best ideas close. They don't want to talk without a signed non-disclosure agreement. They won't share without getting paid. On the other hand, those who are the most successful tend to share their best ideas freely. They realize that anyone with the means will be happy to hire an expert to take care of the details. My mechanic can explain exactly how to fix my car, but it doesn't mean I want to spend a Saturday doing it myself. By trusting me with his most valuable ideas, he illustrates his expertise and wins me over. This it the mindset that gets consumers lining up around the block for your services. With this in mind, the content of your blogs should not be advertorial or, if it is, should be made up of something like 90% helpful posts to 10% advertisements and self-promotions. People don't care about your internal promotions nearly as much as you think they do, so those count as advertisements. Basically anything you write about yourself goes in the self-promo bucket. You can do one of those posts for every nine purely helpful posts that contain no advertisement whatsoever. A ratio of this sort will keep you from violating the principles of helpeting, but don't confuse self-promotion with reach. It's important that you actively pursue getting your blog in front of other people in a regular basis. One of the most important tools for bloggers is building an email list of subscribers who want to read your content. We'll talk more about this in the next couple of sections, but with tools like AWeber and Mailchimp you can automatically send an email to subscribers each time a blog goes live. It's essential to content marketing for you to take advantage of every automatic system you can get your hands on in order to make your helpeting sustainable over the long-term. No matter how committed you are, there will be times when you're too busy and too frustrated with a lack of results to continue. Having automatic systems in place will help make it easier to keep going during these times, and it gives you a margin for periods when the blogs aren't exactly pouring out.

HOW TO RUIN YOUR BLOG

If you go searching for advice for bloggers, you're likely to find a lot on the subject of getting it done in as little time as possible—remember, blogging is more time intensive than many people are prepared for. I take a different tack. I say we should be asking ourselves how we can take more time with our blogs, not less. The world doesn't need more lists of the top four rules for social media or three great leadership tips you can implement today. If people want those lists, there are already a million available just a few clicks away on Google. It's true that these are the headlines that garner the most clicks, and there's nothing wrong with organizing your content in an easy-to-digest format, like a list. Just don't sacrifice quality for quantity. I'm going to say that again: do not sacrifice quality for quantity. A high number of clicks is helpful, but only if people begin to realize your witty headlines actually lead to something worth reading. Instead of spewing out as many words as possible in less time, figure out how you, as a thought leader in your space, can deliver greater value than your competition. Then figure out how to present that value in the most digestible way possible. Most blog posts average 500 words, though there is a movement towards longer pieces. Some writers are successful with 2,000-4,000 word blogs. Try a variety. Better yet, take the space you need, be it long or short. I'm not a fan of writing to a certain target length. It's one thing to target 500 words for a blog or 50,000 for an ebook, but once you decide to write to a rough length, let the piece dictate how many words it should be. Write as clearly and concisely as possible in order to get your point across. One sign of an amateur writer is that they take seven words to say what could be said in four. Many writers try to reduce the total length of their piece by at least 10% in their second draft. Keep in mind that this means your revision process is going to be just as important as, if not more than, your writing process. One simply cannot put out a great piece of writing without any revisions. Even Stephen King heavily revises his books and he's written over 50 consecutive bestsellers totaling millions of words. That's a lot of practice, and a lot of revision.

How you go about revising your work is entirely up to you. One system I find helpful is to write a blog straight through on the first draft without any re-reading or editing. I let my thoughts flow out stream of consciousness. When I'm done, I shelve it for at least a week, usually two. Then I go through and completely rewrite it. It usually takes me twice as long to do the rewrite as it does to write the original piece. After the big rewrite, I like to get feedback from a few people before revising one more time. In this final draft, I'll usually add a few things for clarity and remove some points that didn't add much or wandered off topic. Then I send it to someone else to edit. You can use other people at any point during the whole process, or you can wait till you have a final draft, but whatever you do always have another person do a final edit. Even the most highly skilled writers will miss things in their own writing.

If all of this sounds overwhelming or even impossible, you're not alone.

Like public speaking, most people are intimidated by writing. It's incredibly difficult to stare at a blank page and feel the pressure to fill it up with something fascinating, but there are methods to help you move forward. You'll have to find what works best for you. There are tons of books and blogs that instruct writers to sit and write something, anything, at the same time each day. It's good advice but, honestly, that doesn't work for me. I fare far better if I'm open to ideas when they strike. When an idea comes to mind, I make time to write as soon as possible. I'd rather rearrange my day or take time that evening to write down something I'm excited about than let it wait. I get ten times as much done if I'm excited about an idea and it's fresh in my mind. I'm also in the habit of keeping a list of topics that interest me. When I think of a possible subject for a blog post, I email it to myself and store it in a folder. I can pull that folder up any time and start on whichever topic catches my fancy in the moment. These habits are just me, of course.

Whatever works for you should be your method.

The key is staying open to the possibilities. Blogging ideas can come to you almost daily if you train yourself to be open. What excites you? What pissed you off today? What's wrong in the world or your industry that needs to be fixed? What did an employee do to screw up a new account? What did someone else do to save it? What did a client do to make your life miserable or awesome? This is the stuff of great blogging. Never make the mistake of thinking you have nothing to share. If you have a pulse, you have something worth broadcasting. You just have to reach into that gifted mind of yours and pull it out onto the printed page. That's where ghost writers can really come in handy. They're great at pulling out your ideas and putting them into words. Then they give you the credit because they are, after all, your ideas.

APPLICATION FOR TODAY

Determine what a realistic blogging schedule looks like for you and create a calendar for the entire year with themes and topics. Assign dates and deadlines to everyone who will be contributing at least a month (preferably several) in advance. Then stockpile a couple months' worth of posts and get them scheduled out in advance. Set up an account with Mail Chimp or AWeber if you don't already have one and link it to your blog.

Once you have all your pieces in place, start publishing and keep writing.

HELPETERS IN A SOCIAL WORLD

Social media has emerged as a powerful tool for connecting, building trust and helping people online. It's a complex world of its own, but I've found four basic principles that stand out as the most important when engaging with your audience on social media.

RELATIONSHIPS

Social media is a unique, strong and dynamic tool. While the need for relationships isn't new, some of the instruments we use to build and maintain those relationships have changed. Building an engaged social media community will never happen if the person or organization at the center of that community forgets that it's not all about them. It can't be about selling a book or a widget or building an audience to get more advertisers. Social media starts and ends with relationships. It's obvious how much people matter to many top social media personalities. I think this is the primary reason they're successful. You can attract new people with a giveaway every day, but you won't keep their attention if they sense that all you care about is yourself. So how do we make sure that we're focusing on relationships? This isn't unlike the other relationships we have in our lives. Dating, parenting, friendship—all lasting relationships require caring, consistency, showing interest, listening, engagement, frequency of contact and openness.

GIVING BACK

Giveaways may not sustain your audience, but they are a great way to jumpstart your online presence. They can build a following very quickly. Facebook has opened up new opportunities to host giveaways directly on your fan page. You can also use tools like Rafflecopter to ensure you're compliant with the laws in your area concerning sweepstakes. Common sense dictates that the bigger the prize, the more entries you'll receive. As with all promotions, I advise that you try different tactics and keep track of your results. Constantly hone your approach, repeating the practices that yield the highest return on your investment. Seek feedback from your audience on what they like and don't like, then adjust the next one accordingly. I've noticed that the organizations and personalities who are the most successful with giveaways do a lot of them and talk about them a great deal.

No matter what prize you offer or how often you do giveaways, they're a great way to give something back to your audience. Just remember that a ton of new followers doesn't necessarily equal engagement with you or your brand. You have a small window of opportunity to bring your new followers into your community before they abandon you for another brand that's more engaging.

YOU DON'T HAVE TO BE OUTGOING

Many people assume that successful socialprenuers are of the outgoing, gregarious type. In my experience, most aren't. Many top personalities I've spoken to identify as private people who are more introverted than extroverted. Despite their introversion, these personalities make an effort to stay engaged with their online community by spending a little time each day commenting on a few of their audience members' profiles and responding to emails, tweets and comments. Some share a lot about their families, posting pictures of their children and telling stories about private family events. Others keep private details to themselves. There are plenty of successful social media personalities on both sides of the spectrum, so decide for yourself how comfortable you are sharing personal information. No matter how open you are, always be private with certain details, like where you go jogging in the morning. The more followers you gain, the more of a target you become. Choose your level of comfort, but be smart about where to draw the line.

YOUR COMMUNITY IS FILLED WITH PEOPLE

It's easy to forget that there's a real person on the other side of that profile page. When a face pops up on the screen, it's tempting to think of them as a statistic. One more tweet. One more comment. One more share. But that picture or comment represents a real person with a life and a history and a legacy of their own. They have goals, hopes, dreams, fears, problems and joys, some which are familiar to you but many that are unique to that person. We can benefit from the diversity of our audience if we're willing to. The perspectives, backgrounds and knowledge of our community are great resources for personal growth. Get to know the people in your community. Find out where your journey intersects with theirs and celebrate the differences. Like most things in life, we get from social media what we put into it. It's a lot of work, but the reward can be huge. Invest in your community and you'll build a tremendous platform of supporters who will stay with you over many years.

APPLICATION FOR TODAY

How can you make a change to your social media plan to reflect these four principles? Come up with at least one tangible to-do that will help you better engage your audience.

EMAIL ETIQUETTE

Though social media is a nifty way to stay in touch with people, email is still king for getting your message in front of an audience. Facebook has the power to change their system a million times, maybe even charging you someday to send messages to people who have liked your page—oh wait, that's right. They already did that. But email? Email you own. No one can change the algorithm for how your emails are going to be displayed or who will see them. It's between you and the recipient. Since email is so powerful, and so commonly abused, it's important to get it right. Email etiquette is essential to succeeding with helpeting. There are basically two major components of email etiquette: sending emails one by one to your personal contacts and email blasting to your readers through services like AWeber.

PERSONAL EMAILS

When you email personal contacts keep it short, as short as possible. Clarity and brevity always win out. The longer the email, the less likely someone is to respond. If they do respond they'll take far longer to do so. People generally reply quickly to things they can do quickly. If they can give you a one-word answer, they might do that on their phone while they're in line to order lunch. If it requires much more thought, they're going to relegate it to their get-to-later list, which often means it won't get done at all. If you have a lot of points to make in an email and need to use some length, split up the message into easily digested parts. Bold big ideas so your reader can scan the message and still get the point. Or split the email up into smaller messages and send them out separately over time. Not only will this allow people to take in your information a little bit at a time, it gives you another reason to follow-up with them more often and stay a little more top of mind.

If you create a clear question or call to action in your email, you're more likely to get a response.

Be direct and clear about what you want your reader to do. Do you need an answer to a question? Make it obvious, even if you have to put your question in bold print. Just please, please, please don't get carried away. The moment you use bold, italics and underlining on the same sentence you just put in red and blue, you lose credibility and a huge portion of your audience is now too busy thinking, "Get an editor," to even notice what you're asking for.

Start with the most important items first. Think of your email like a news article—you don't bury the lead in the last paragraph. People should know most of what they need to know just from the subject line. The email content should become less and less important as it moves down the length of your message. Any pleasantries should be in the last line. As much as people might like to have you hope they're having a great day, they don't want to waste time reading this in the first sentence. You might mean well, but you're taking up their valuable time. I like to save my greetings for the sign off, just above my signature.

Your signature is a great tool that you shouldn't waste. This is your chance to get an important message across to a wide variety of people in a repeatable way. You should also include 2-4 links to important websites that you want to promote, such as your social media accounts or a landing page with valuable information. I also like to put in a line about my niche, a short version of my 30 second pitch or another advertisement. If you do this, avoid any heavy pitching. Your signature isn't the place for an ad as much as for a nice reminder of what you do and how your reader can get involved. This is your chance to keep this message top of mind for every single person you email. I'm often surprised by how often people mention my signature to me when we meet for the first time. Even if you don't see it, people are reading those signatures. And when there's a long email chain with lots of people CC'd, it's included in all of those emails—loads of exposure that you might as well leverage. Some people create their signatures with fancy formatting and pictures, but I tend to avoid this. Mainly because pictures show up as attachments in a lot of email programs and often get cut out. I lean toward simple formatting, using color or bold print for things I want to stand out. Even here, however, I prefer simplicity to a hot mess of formatting. Simplicity says confidence, efficiency and professionalism. Too much formatting says desperate for attention.

HOW MUCH IS TOO MUCH?

The frequency of your messaging is an important part of email etiquette and each relationship requires a different approach. My default is no more than once a week and I often do once a month if I'm just following up with a resource to let someone know I'm thinking of them. With really influential people I tend to limit my emails to once or twice a year and give a lot of thought to making sure my email adds value. There are exceptions, of course. If someone needs something from me by the end of the week but isn't responding, I'll email as often as every day, but only after I've been invited to. Even daily emails don't guarantee a response, though. When people don't respond, and this happens more often than not, I try to tweak my approach. Sometimes I'll try texting, calling, sending a Facebook message or tweeting directly at someone. The most effective way to get in touch depends on the person. Usually it coincides with where they receive the least communication. If their inbox is full but they rarely get phone calls, the phone might be the best way to reach them, plus they might appreciate the change. Sometimes it's just easier to get in touch with someone's assistant. If that's the case, build a relationship with that person and remember they are just as important as the person you're trying to reach. Always respect these gatekeepers as if they were the king or queen, because as far as you're concerned, they are. Who doesn't appreciate respect? These are people who appreciate being regarded as more than a gatekeeper for someone they are constantly told is more important than they are. In fact, if you give the assistant your attention and respect simply for who they are and not what they can do for you, you'll stand out from most of the people trying to reach their boss and you'll be far more likely to actually reach their boss in the end. Helpeting does not overlook assistants and support staff.

EMAIL BLASTING AND YOUR LIST

The first thing to consider with email blasts is the email service you'll use. AWeber, Mailchimp and Constant Contact are currently the top three providers. Whenever you email a lot of people with the same message you stand a high chance of being labeled as spam, but these services have gone to great lengths to ensure that their messages get delivered. Some are free for small users, others cost between \$20 and \$100 a month or more depending on the list size, but this is money well spent. These services manage unsubscribes and generate reports to help you know which campaigns are doing better than others. No matter which service you go with, though, you're going to need an email list. It's a major part of any helpeting campaign. First things first: do not purchase email lists. Spamming is annoying and ineffective, I don't care what people tell you. Yes, it works for Viagra knockoffs, but do you really want to be lumped in with that lot? It's really not that hard to build your own email list, especially if you have an audience of people who already like what you do. It takes time, but we already know helpeting takes time. In the end, a strong list of supporters who actually read your emails, and possibly even look forward to getting them, is the best possible path toward growing your platform.

If you're starting from scratch, I usually advise that you get a one time opportunity to add everyone you know to your list. After adding them, send an email that says that you did, why you thought they might want to be on the list and how they can unsubscribe easily. Most people you know will understand this as a one-time affair, but if they unsubscribe don't add them again. And you really can't do this more than once every five years or so without annoying your friends and family.

Make it easy to sign up for your list whenever you speak, in the back of your books and any other place you can think of where you'll encounter people who might want to hear from you from time to time. In order to grow your list you need to make it easy and attractive to be on it. One of the best ways is to have a non-annoying pop up that offers something valuable in exchange for signing up. You could do a giveaway for new subscribers, offer a free ebook or a series of emails that offer a new top tip once a week for ten weeks. Don't skimp on this giveaway. It's important that your offer is valuable in order to get subscribers and keep them past the first email.

Once you've built your email list, it's time to start sending emails. Ideally you have a blog packed with high quality content that you'll want to send out. AWeber offers the best choice for automatically sending emails from your blog, a really useful feature when it comes to automating your helpeting. All the major email blasting services offer the ability to set up automatic responses, so you can set up your list and send an automatic email either immediately after someone subscribes or later on. This is a great tool to take advantage of because once you set it up, you don't have to do anything to keep it going. You might have a series of tips that go out over time, resources to help your subscribers, a question to engage your audience or even an offer for your services (remember to keep this one scarce —your unsubscribe rate will increase with the frequency of your advertising).

The key is to think about whether or not your audience would be

happy to receive your email.

Make the value high and you should have minimal unsubscribes. If you're delivering value, don't get too upset when someone bows out of your list. No matter what you do, no matter how good your emails are, you will receive unsubscribes, guaranteed. It's just a natural part of our overly busy world. I've also noticed that the larger your list gets, the lower your response rates will be as a percentage of subscribers. For example, a list of 500 might have an open rate of 30% and a click rate of 8%, but a good open rate for a list of 5,000 will be 20% while clicks drop to 4%. The average click rate for very large lists is around 1% and the open rate hovers around 5-10%. This can vary widely depending on how well you've managed your list and what kind of people are in your target market.

I often advise clients to set up multiple lists that subscribers are automatically subscribed to. One should be an everything list. People on this list will get everything you send, including an email for all your new blog entries. A second list should be for the weekly or monthly group. This would be a newsletter and a recap of posts for the last week or month, respectively. The final list is an occasional list that only gets used for major events and top posts. I might send to this list once a quarter. It's important to send emails to all of your lists at least once a quarter because email addresses become stale as people abandon or change them. It looks bad to your email service and the people who track spam if you send to old emails no longer in use. Those emails should be automatically cleaned out by your email service if you send to them regularly. I find that sending emails on Tuesday, Wednesday or Thursday at noon PST is the best time because it reaches all the U.S. markets during prime working hours that aren't as busy as the morning hours. However, if you find that another time works best for your purposes —perhaps you're not even targeting readers in the U.S.—then by all means, adapt your email schedule. No matter what approach you take to personal emails and email blasting, test and adjust your approach. Every audience and content creator is different. You might find that sending one email early every Saturday morning or that an email every day works best for you. We often assume that everyone else wants what we want, but what really matters is what gets the best results. So test and adapt accordingly.

APPLICATION FOR TODAY

If you don't already have one, sign up for an account with an email blasting service and get started on building your list. Create a free resource that you can give away as a tool for building it up and set up some automatic responses to automate your helpeting.

EBOOKS

Authoring your own ebook can be transformative for your career or business. Even though millions of people are jumping on the ebook bandwagon, there's still room for you, especially if you do it better than others. The thing is, great content will always be in demand. It doesn't matter if every single person on the planet has an ebook, the best ones will rise to the top and help establish those who wrote them as leaders in their thought space. That's why today, more than ever, it's critical for you to develop your ideas and execute your content projects at a higher level than anyone around you. It's your only hope of standing out.

One powerful thing about ebooks is that they don't have to be a certain length, even if you want to create a print version. Short ebooks can be printed without being mistaken for a children's book. Make the font a little larger, add a little more white space around the margins and shrink the overall page size. Then own the fact that it's short. Tell people on the cover or in the intro that you've created something easy to digest on a short flight. Make the short length a feature, not a weakness. I believe firmly in the power of publishing any ebook in a printed format, an easy and inexpensive process thanks to services like Amazon's Createspace or even Ingram Spark if you want a hard cover. Releasing your book in print will automatically separate you from many of your competitors. If you don't want to do all the work, hire someone. Just check out their portfolio and make sure their work is on par with the quality of a major release.

The most sellable books for helpeting have a system.

If you don't already have one, you need to come up with a system that anyone can apply and then provide step-by-step instructions. This may seem like you're giving away your farm, but you're actually illustrating how much you know about a topic your reader is interested in. Many people will try it on their own and if you're serious about helping others that's a good thing. But many readers won't want to go it alone. They're too busy with their core strengths and, since you've been so generous with your content and proven that you're the expert, why not look you up and hire you to do the work for them? Keep in mind when picking your topic that it's important your book fills a gap in the available resources. You're solving a big problem that people care about. It's helpful to blatantly point out a problem you see in the world or the marketplace, the lack of resources for solving it and the fact that you're setting out to fill that need by writing a book about your system, a system which happens to be a great way to address the problem.

Within your book, I highly recommend you lean heavily on stories. If you can replace a list of bullet points with a story, do it. This is the difference between watching a movie and hearing the summary. The movie causes you to change or learn something because it embeds it within a story, making it both entertaining and engrossing. Malcolm Gladwell is the gold standard for communicating ideas through story. If you're setting out to write your own ebook, do yourself a favor and read his work. You know the 10,000 hour rule that's been cited everywhere? That was Malcolm's doing. He said mastery comes after 10,000 hours of practice. Multiple studies have asserted that this is not universal, but Malcolm argued his point so convincingly with stories about the Beatles and chess champions, his ideas have ingrained themselves into our culture. That's the power of story. Okay, so that's sort of a negative example of the power of story, but there are countless positive examples as well. Movies, songs, poems, orators, novels and even two friends over coffee show time and again that story can move us to feel, to change and to act.

It's true that it's what's on the inside that counts. Now that you have a book brimming with helpful insight, let's talk about the outside. Despite our mothers' warnings never to judge a book by its cover, we do it anyway. In terms of achieving your end goal, your book's cover is as important as the content. Not only should you hire someone to design it for you, you should hire someone whose work is of a quality that rivals that of major publishers. In fact, if possible, hire someone who works for a major publisher. You should expect to pay about $1,000 for work of this caliber. You could get it done for as little as $100 if you're really, really good at spotting and sourcing talented designers, but if you have the budget your cover is worth the investment.

One thing that will really set you up well for marketing your book is a book trailer. If you haven't seen one, they're sort of like a movie trailer, but for a book. For most nonfiction titles they're either animated or contain an interview that communicates the problem, the importance of solving it and how the book is going to get it done. The trailers often, like the marketing copy, give away the best secrets. This is important because, just like in your emails, you don't want to bury the hook. Making promises won't work—that's what people do when they don't really have anything good to offer. Give away your very best ideas and people will want to read how you explain and apply them.

Pricing is the tricky part of e-publishing. There are three basic strategies for helpeting publishing, each one maximizing a different value: number of readers, profit or reputation. On one hand, $2.99 is the best price point for maximum profit. You can find ways to get Amazon to make your book permanently free, which will maximize the number of readers. However, those readers may not be in your target market and are far more likely to give you negative reviews. (Funny how the people who get something for free are the most likely to tear it apart, huh?) The third strategy for pricing is to mark it $9.99 or more. This makes it seem more valuable and looks more like a big publisher's release, since larger publishers charge $9.99 or more for their new releases. You won't sell a lot of books this way, but when people check you out they'll perceive that you're a high quality source. Whatever your price point, selling books is hard. You shouldn't expect to sell many or make a profit from your ebook unless you have an excited audience that numbers north of 100,000. But you can sell some printed copies whenever you speak. And better yet, you can give away your book as an introduction point to your company. If this is your primary strategy, then list the book with a high price and get copies to give out when you meet people. You can also give copies to people who want to promote you, such as advocates and colleagues. Believe it or not, giving physical copies of your book away is harder than most people think. You actually have to pay to give your book away, ether by advertising it on a social site like

Facebook or by paying websites to feature it. There are a lot of ways to distribute a free ebook online, including through your email list. If you want to get a ton of exposure you can use sites such as bookbub.com, which charges you something like $100-$200 to email their millions of email subscribers and let them know that your book is free (there are other sites that aren't as big but will still give you some exposure). Bookbub gets a lot of submissions so your book must meet certain requirements, like a minimum number of positive reviews, and even then you may not be accepted. Keep trying and they could eventually pick your book. Just know that getting reviews is even more difficult than selling your book. You can beg your best friend to review your book and she may still forget. The best system I've found for this is bloggers and goodreads.com. You can reach out to bloggers directly and ask them to review your book if you give them a free copy. If you can, do this through an assistant so that it looks like you're not the run of the mill self-pub author. Most individual bloggers don't accept review submissions from self-published authors because the quality is generally low. So make sure your quality is high. See that you have professional design and editing and that your content is top notch. You can hire a publisher to help you with this. You might consider putting someone over your work and hiring a high quality, experienced editor who will be direct enough to help you develop your content to the demanding level of the larger publishing world. The other way of getting reviews is through goodreads.com. You can list a printed version of your book as a giveaway on their site. Once you list a giveaway, people will sign up to get it and many of them will add your book to their to-read list. You can have your assistant email these people and offer them a free ebook if they will agree to review it. Once they've published their review on Goodreads, ask them to copy it into Amazon.

It's possible to create a valuable

ebook that isn't extremely long.

If you have a series of PowerPoint slides that you've used to deliver value to your target market, you can have a designer turn those into a book, a tangible thing to hand out to clients and people you meet. Just make sure it's helpful and not marketing in disguise. Gather your ideas into an easily implemented system that you can communicate with graphics and concise wording.

APPLICATION FOR TODAY

Create a list of possible topics for an ebook. Identify what is doable for the length and format you like best and what topic would be most helpful to your target audience. You might consider asking a few of your ideal customers directly for their input on what kind of ebook they would find valuable, given your expertise in the field. Create a plan to complete the book either with internal resources or by hiring someone to help you.

LIVE! FROM ANYWHERE

Hosting live online events has never been easier and, as technology improves, it's becoming an even better solution for resourcing your target market.

There are a number of benefits to live online events over live in-person events. One is that no one besides you has to know how many people are watching. Nothing is worse than doing a presentation for an empty room, but online no one knows that the virtual room is empty. And, let's face it, everyone does a presentation for an empty room from time to time, especially when we're just getting started. Another benefit is cost. It's easy to have guests join you from around the world by logging in rather than paying for their travel to come to a single location. The same is true for your audience. Even if your target market is limited geographically, it's nice for your audience to be able to get online during their lunch or between appointments rather than having to drive across town. And it's so easy and cheap to set up online events that there's really no reason not to be doing them regularly. Videocasts are superior to podcasts, too. It's so easy to do video now, why not add that to your offering? People don't have to be watching the video to listen to it, but there is something more engaging about making your video feed available. And for those audience members who would rather listen in the car or at the gym, you can easily turn your video feeds into an audio only podcast. In my opinion, Google hangout is the best solution available today for hosting. It doesn't put any sign-ups or funky webforms between your audience and your show, plus it's live, available anywhere and automatically becomes a YouTube video after you finish. If you have advertising set up, you can also make a little money depending on your traffic stats.

There are a number of formats for an online show, the most common being a webinar. The problem I have with webinars is that they sound boring, but maybe that's just because most of them are. They usually involve product demos and sales pitches and long winded people making presentations. I prefer a roundtable discussion about a particular topic. I like to have people interrupting each other and chasing rabbit holes because that can lead to some of the most helpful, unplanned content. Plus, you and your guests have to prepare for hours to do a good webinar. When it's an online discussion led by someone adept at pulling out and facilitating good conversation, almost no preparation is required. This is good news if you decide to host it yourself, which is a great way to get influencers involved with your mission. I've found it's a pretty easy ask to get someone influential to join you for a 30-60 minute Google hangout, a lot easier than getting them to write a blog for you or even meet them in person. Make it all about them and tell them you're going to give them a chance to build their platform.

If you do decide to host an online show, think through in detail how you want to structure it. The format I like to use starts with a short, visual intro that presents the logos of the organizations involved in that episode, with music and animation. Putting time into this small detail shows your audience that you take them seriously. I also like to create lower third banners for each guest. These can look customized and allow your guests the opportunity to build their platform by mentioning their social media handles and websites. After the show starts, I have a host introduce the show and ask the audience to get involved by tweeting their questions using a custom hashtag. We also use a Facebook comments plugin on the page to create a question form, giving our audience another option for voicing their questions. Your host can monitor these questions or, if possible, it's helpful to have an assistant, staff member or volunteer monitor them for your host and text or email him/her the best questions. Before we even do the show, I usually ask the guests for some softball questions we can ask during the show to help guide the conversation toward whatever they think would be helpful for their audience. My team and I also have some stock questions of our own prepared for the same purpose. We rarely get to these questions, however, because the best shows happen when everyone is talking off the cuff and having a genuine conversation. I encourage guests to laugh together and loosen up. No one wants to sit through a carefully scripted conversation among a bunch of people who seem to take themselves too seriously.

The show intro is followed by brief introductions of the guests so that your viewers know these who these people are and that they are authorities in their respective areas. Then we dive into the content, and we do so as soon as possible. People don't have time for a drawn out introduction. They're watching the show to learn something. In the middle of the show, at least once or twice, we again invite people to be a part of what's going on by sending their questions to us. We usually point out that most content today is one directional, like conferences and blogging, whereas this is their big chance to get their specific questions answered by an expert. We always thank people for asking questions when we use them in the show and we mention their handle if we have it. We tweet our thanks directly to these people as well, and include a link to the show that can boost traffic if these tweets are shared.

As we get closer to the end of the show, we warn our audience that we'll be wrapping up soon. I learned to do that so it doesn't feel like we lost track of time and have to end abruptly. Then, as a last segment we ask each guest to share one last thought as well as the best way to follow-up with them. This is the only sales pitch I allow on a show and even then it's not really a pitch as much as a way to help your audience. If they like what our guest has to say, we want to make it easy for them to find more where that came from. It also gives the guests a shot at a little self-promotion, which is the best way to thank them for their time. We usually close the show, not by promoting ourselves or our company, but by asking people to pencil in the show on their calendars and join us next time. We broadcast our show live at the same time and place each week or month so people know when it's coming.

You can have the same people join you regularly, though I like bringing in new guests a lot because it expands your tribe. You should expect your guests to promote your show, but each one is going to do so differently. The bigger an audience your guests have, the harder it is to get those guests to promote your show. I usually treat all guests the same, no matter their following, and provide pre-written tweets for them a week ahead of time with instructions on how often to tweet and when. I ask nicely and make it as easy as possible, but I don't get upset if they don't. However, if a guest doesn't show any interest in promoting the show, I usually don't ask them back because I want people who are into what we're doing. Sure, it's nice to have a big name but it's better to have a tribe of influencers who are into your gig. In general, we have three guests on each show. With the host, that makes four people total. Any less and you run the risk of dead spots where the conversation dies. A lot of that depends on the experience of your guests, of course. If you have a really dynamic speaker and a list of questions ready to go, you could just do a Q&A with a no more than your host and a single guest, but I prefer the conversation that takes place between four or five people for the sake of audience engagement. We also try to match the level of the guest. If we have a really high profile person coming on, I try to get them to bring a couple of their peers, or I reach out and get some of the high profile people in my network to join us. Usually if you can get one, it's a lot easier to get a few more to join. It's unwise to pair really influential guests with less influential guests because I've found that people will just defer to the more famous personality. After all, it's hard to talk over someone who has a million twitter followers when you have 500. People tend to assume the better known guest knows more and people would rather hear what they have to say, even if that isn't true. It's also just the practical matter that people with a large following tend to have a high level of material to offer. So if you put them with someone who's just starting out, you're going to make the less experienced one look bad by comparison, even if they have good ideas to contribute. Their ideas, and the ability they have to communicate them, won't look good in direct comparison to the more experienced, more influential person. And finally, big time people usually hang out with big time people. They're used to being the center of attention, for better or worse. If you put them with other big time people, they expect to share the platform.

After the show is over, we always send out a follow-up to our guests with not only our thanks but an exposure report that shows how well the show performed stats-wise compared to other shows. I want my guests to know that we care about getting them in front of people and promoting their brand.

There's something great about a regular live

event for your organization.

It builds both your audience and the influencers who are in your circle, plus it adds an energy to your offering that I haven't found through any other means.

APPLICATION FOR TODAY

Make a list of topics for shows that you can host that would help your audience. What influencers in your circle could you invite to be on the show with you? Do you have a potential host, someone great at facilitating conversation and keeping things lighthearted? Come up with a date for your first show and create a content calendar that includes at least one show per month.

MAKING CONNECTIONS

Making connections between people is the lynchpin of networking and one of the best ways to help your target market. It's something almost anyone can do easily and quickly, it requires a fairly small amount of time and can be incredibly helpful. That's when it's done the right way. Done the wrong way, making connections becomes a liability that can do serious harm to your relationships, reputation and results. It's one of the most misunderstood and abused aspects of helpeting, so we're going to spend some time breaking it down.

Connections have to be

helpful for everyone involved.

It's not about numbers, it's about quality. Though making connections can be a time effective way of serving people, doing it right requires a significant investment from you. Take the time to think through the connections you make and resist the urge to connect random people on a whim or because you figure they'll get along. This alone will go a long way toward increasing the quality of your connections. Your goal should be that when you offer someone a connection, they drop everything and follow-up on it. They'll do this when you've built a reputation for making strategic referrals. Even if you don't hit that every time, making it your goal will take care of a lot of the pitfalls of connecting people. The opposite would be building a reputation that causes people to trash your referrals, which certainly happens with bad introductions. People connect you in their mind to the people you introduce them to. So when you introduce someone to the guy who didn't even show up for the appointment, had nothing in common with them, talked about himself the whole time or tried to get them to buy into some MLM program, your name takes the hit. It's hard to recover once you've got a reputation for giving bad referrals. There are some practical steps you can take to keep from making bad referrals. One thing I'm careful to do is make sure both parties want an introduction before I make it. When I'm connecting people on two sides of a sales transaction, like someone looking for a home and a real estate agent, I ask the customer side if they'd like me to introduce them. The more busy and influential the customer, the more vital it is to ask this question. If they're at the top of their career and running a large operation, they're likely to be hit up constantly, but that doesn't mean they don't want to meet people who can help them out. A quick email is all it takes. I describe the person I'd like to introduce them to, pitching them as well as I can, and ask if an introduction would be helpful at this time. If they say no but maybe later, I make a note to check in with them later, at a time they've said would be more helpful.

Here's how this looks in real life. I know a woman, we'll call her Romy, who runs a large manufacturing company with over 200 employees. She founded the company ten years ago and has had tremendous growth. When I last met with her she described a few business issues she was dealing with. I made a note of these issues and later called up a friend of mine, a CEO, who coaches business leaders at various levels. He has a peer group of CEOs and owners of large manufacturing companies similar in size to Romy's. I didn't tell him Romy's name since I didn't have permission to share her issues publicly, but I listed the issues she was facing and asked my friend if he would be able to help her and how well she would fit into one of his groups. It sounded like a great match so I emailed Romy and told her all about my friend's coaching and services and asked if she would like an introduction. She responded that she normally would but she was swamped, so maybe in six months. I made a note in my calendar to ask her again in six months and sure enough, six months later she was ready to meet with the coach. I introduced them over coffee and soon they were engaged in a long standing coaching arrangement that has lasted to this day.

Usually when dealing with a customer/supplier intro, you can assume that the person on the supplier side is going to be happy to meet with the customer. If you know what kind of customers that person is looking for, this is an even safer assumption. Even still, it's a nice gesture to give the supplier a profile of the company and ask if it would be a good fit. Be honest with them. Does the customer have any downsides? Have you heard they're a little slow paying their bills? If so, let your supplier contact know this and decide for themselves if they want to pursue the relationship. They usually will, and they'll think highly of you for considering them to the point that you're helping them vet great customers. Again, it's not about quantity. It's about quality. I would rather have a single great introduction per year than a hundred bad ones. In fact, if anyone gave me hundred bad introductions I would beg them to stop. Bad introductions are a waste of time for everyone and because of that they violate the principles behind helpeting.

People who are great at connecting others are always on the lookout for introduction opportunities.

They go into meetings looking for ways to make great connections, even more than they're trying to get business or something for themselves. When the opportunity presents itself, they ask questions like,

"Who does your payroll?" "What's your plan for expansion in the next quarter?" "What kinds of problems are you facing?" "What's the one thing you could improve to increase employee happiness or sales or profit or retention or anything else?" People who think like this are worth their weight in gold to their relationships. They go out of their way to make helpful introductions to people they know and meet and are consequently known as incredibly helpful people. These are the sort who are never short of friends and rarely find themselves in need of anything because of the huge number of people they've helped over the years. Keep in mind that the power of referrals, and the reason the whole system works, is that you're lending a bit of your trust to help form a new relationship. Think of it as seed capital. You're investing the trust you have with both of these people who don't know each other, vouching for your belief that they will benefit from knowing each other. They decide, hopefully, that if you trust this other person then they can too. And just like a bank loan you co-signed on, if the person you refer doesn't show up or acts like a jerk, you're on the hook. You're going to lose a bit of trust with the person you referred that person to. You don't want this to happen, so make sure you invest your connections well. On the flip side, when you invest well you reap well. This is the same with connections. When you make a good connection, good will and increased trust comes back to you from both parties that is even more valuable than the amount of time and trust you invested in the relationship.

This is where many people simply miss the point with connections. They hoard their network, keeping it close and secret. They think of it as a finite asset that they have to hold onto so they can't lose it. Connections and networking is the polar opposite. The more you use it, if you use it properly, the stronger and more valuable it becomes. Some people's networks are literally worth billions of dollars. You don't build a billion dollar network by hiding your connections and never introducing anyone.

APPLICATION FOR TODAY

It's hard to keep track of your connections in your head. If you don't have one already, sign up for a simple CRM software like Highrise (a great solution for a lot of people). This allows you to track interactions with people, make notes about following up and keep track of who introduced you to whom.

ACING THE ONE-ON-ONE

One-on-one meetings are an essential ingredient to any helpeter's mix. I've learned a few tricks over the years that I'd like to pass on for how to maximize your ability to help people and get the most out of your meetings.

When I first meet someone, say at a networking social or even a cold introduction, and I'm not sure who they are exactly or what I might be able to do for them, I like to start by setting up a 30 minute phone call. There are a number of great things about this first step. First, you can do the call in your car driving between appointments, so you're capitalizing on your car time. Second, if you can't help this person, which is going to happen more often than not, you haven't wasted more than a half hour of their time. Third, by making the meeting shorter it forces everyone involved to be a little more efficient with their time. There's less time for small talk and the shorter timeframe will force you to get down to it faster. Finally, 30 minutes seems to be just the right amount of time to find out what someone is all about and how you might be able to engage with them. If the 30 minute phone call goes well and I think there are some ways I might be able to significantly help this person, I set up a face-to-face meeting.

In person meetings can also be as short as 30 minutes and have similar benefits to that initial phone call. However, an hour is the standard for most meetings. I've also heard of people having a lot of success with 45 minutes because it allows some buffer in your day and a chance to get to your next appointment if it's nearby. In some cases I go as long as 90 minutes if I really want time to dive in with someone. I only do this after I've met with the person a number of times and can be relatively sure that it's going to be a good use of their time. During any meeting, no matter how long, you should spend more than half of the time talking about the other person. If they're polite and interested in you, they'll insist that you talk about yourself as well. Even if they don't insist, you should volunteer a least some information about yourself. If you don't, it can lead to a sort of awkward moment when they realize they've been talking about themselves the whole time. Plus, you want them to know about your areas of experience and what you might be able to do for them. That way, if you miss the connection between something they need and what you have to offer, they are free to make that connection themselves and ask for your help. For this reason, I sometimes start a meeting by talking about myself for at least 5 minutes. I want them to know that I have something to offer and build my credibility. This is one of the only situations where bragging isn't really bragging. It's like a bio. There are times when you shouldn't hide what you've done and if you do it comes off like false modesty anyway, which doesn't help anyone.

Everyone wants to be understood. Everyone

wants to be heard.

Humans are all hardwired to seek connection and listening is a way of connecting to someone. Not just any listening, though. Present listening. You aren't multitasking. You aren't thinking about your next appointment. You are listening intently to the person across from you. This is another reason I do my first 30 minute appointment over the phone while I'm driving. I can't write notes or check my email. Granted, driving itself takes some of my focus, but the person on the other end of the line has most of my attention. Once that conversation is over, subsequent meetings happen face-to-face and when you're in such a meeting, no one else in the world matters more than the person sitting across from you. The odd thing about listening instead of talking is that when you focus your attention on understanding others, they find you more interesting. The less you say about yourself, the more they remember you as an interesting person, a likable person, a person they enjoy being around.

The only exception that seems acceptable to most people is when a spouse or child calls or texts during an appointment. The majority of us respect anyone who always puts their family first, and it's important for your family to know they can get ahold of you anytime. So if your wife or husband calls, don't hesitate to politely ask for a moment and shift your focus to your family. Other than that, you're zeroed in, which is easier when you're not worried about the time. I prefer to leave a buffer between my appointments of at least thirty minutes. This is a great time to catch up on a few emails and write to-do notes from my last meeting, plus it allows me to relax about the time. I want to be the person who has all the time in the world and to allow the other person to decide when it's time to end the appointment. It's a great way to show them how much they mean to you and it presents you as a very put together, well-managed individual. We aren't drawn to harried people who are always running from one thing to the next, people who seem out of control. We're drawn to people who seem to have everything together and we wonder how they get so much done since every time we meet they have nothing on their mind besides us. That's a great feeling to have and it's a great feeling to give other people.

At the very least, you should follow-up on all your appointments by the end of the day. It's too easy to forget if you push it to the next day. I always send a follow-up email to every person I meet, not only thanking them for the appointment but adding a little value and letting them know what I'm going to do next and when I plan to do it. I keep it short, leaving the opportunity to send more emails with more info down the road. These are opportunities to keep top of mind later and you don't want to inundate people with a ton of information when you can give it to them on a drip campaign.

Never try to sell something in your one-on-one

meetings unless specifically asked.

Even then I try to put it off by letting them know I'd rather just get to know them better before I get into how we might be able to help each other. Word of warning here—this can be taken too far and come off as coy or a waste of time. Try not to cross that line. At some point, people just want you to tell them straight up what you can do for them and how much it costs. Just do your best to put that off as long as possible so you can gather more information before you get into the weeds.

APPLICATION FOR TODAY

Who are you meeting with next? How will you plan your meeting agenda to ensure that at least 50% of the meeting is about them? How can you rearrange your schedule to allow for more buffer time between meetings? What opportunities do you have for short phone call meetings? Who can you set up in those slots? Make a few adjustments if necessary, reach out to a few people each week to schedule into your 30 minute driving slots and make a plan for how to take control of your meetings to make them about the people sitting across from you.

MORE WAYS TO HELP

Besides the methods we've already covered, there are a few more ways I've found to help people that might benefit you. These include sending an article of interest, compiling lists of resources, sharing helpful comparisons between competing products or services and creating or curating inspirational picture quotes.

SENDING AN ARTICLE OR BOOK OF INTEREST

If you're browsing the web or flipping through a magazine and you stumble upon an article you find helpful, make a note of it somewhere so you can easily find it again. Then when you need to follow-up with a potential customer, you can go to this list and find an article that would benefit them. You can do the same thing by giving them or mailing them a book. Though that's obviously more expensive, it makes a really good impression. Some people carry around a trunk of books and bring one to a second or third meeting as a gift. Whether it's an article or a book, ideally you've put a bit of thought into how the content relates to the customer. You want to be able to say something like, "I remember you were having a tough time finding a new employee and I found this article that offers some good insight." This shows that you were listening, that you were thinking of them and that you cared enough to go through the trouble of finding and sending the article or buying the book.

COMPILING LISTS OF RESOURCES

You don't have to create a resource to be helpful in sharing it. Some people have had great success pooling lists or folders of resources that they use as a giveaway or something they can send potential clients who might benefit. This is the same idea as sending an article of interest, but it's that idea on steroids. Instead of just one article, you give someone an entire library of resources. These can also be creative, such as a folder filled with royalty free images or music (just make sure you have permission to share them). You can compile any resource that's helpful to your audience and share it in a way that shows how much you care, illustrating your commitment to putting your clients' needs first.

MAKING COMPARISONS BETWEEN COMPETING OPTIONS

People have been using product comparisons and reviews for some time to increase SEO and organic web traffic. Often, those giving the reviews or comparisons are set up as affiliates with all the companies they're reviewing, so no matter which one you decide to buy, they get a percentage. It generally goes against helpeting principles to profit from making a referral. You can profit far more by simply helping people and having that return to you in the form of more core business. If you make a note of not making any money off a referral, it also shows your commitment to providing an unbiased opinion.

Implementing this helpeting tactic is pretty straightforward. Find a few products or services that are likely to be helpful to your target market and do comparisons or reviews of them on your website. Remember, doing this as quickly as possible isn't in your best interest. Far better to do less of these and spend more time making sure they're more comprehensive than the reviews already out there if you're going to have any hope of cutting through the clutter. It's also helpful to be first on the scene. Those who review and compare products or services early are more likely to benefit in the form of organic traffic. Be on the lookout for trends in your marketplace and move quickly to review or compare when something new comes up.

PICTURE QUOTES

Pictures quotes are a great way to engage an audience through social media and blogging. It's a lot easier to like a picture quote than an article link because it takes just a few seconds to read it and approve of the content. Remember that most people don't want to like or share something unless they've seen the whole thing and they certainly don't want to share something they don't agree with.

Picture quotes are easy to make, too. Just find a pool of great stock images, have a designer create a template that includes the quote, the name of the person who said it and space for a link to your website or blog. These can be your own quotes or they can come from someone else. Keep track of what works best and do more of it. This is a great way to grow your social media following as well, because when people share the quotes they expose more people to your brand.

APPLICATION FOR TODAY

Decide which of these four tools is the best approach for you to serve your audience. Then make a plan to start implementing it into your regular schedule. Buy the books, find the articles, do the reviews or make the picture quotes. Have them at the ready so you don't get caught without something helpful for your audience.

BE GENUINE TO YOURSELF

I shouldn't have taken that last run. In the fading Rocky Mountain dusk, I could barely make out the choppy slush as I sailed over it, struggling to maintain control of my skins as I raced to catch up to my brother Jeff. Cabin lights flickered orange like frozen fireflies lurking in the woods around the base of Sundance Ski Resort. We had, rather foolishly as brothers of all ages sometimes do, decided to race down the gorge despite the poor conditions. As I rounded the corner into a black diamond called Cotton Mouth, the edge of my ski caught in a groove. An eye blink later my head smacked the ice. Jeff hockey-stopped a few feet above where I fell, spraying me with snow. I lay there on my side for a while, listening to the ringing as he called the snow patrol. Fortunately I was wearing a helmet, but the concussion gummed up my grey matter for months.

My family makes the 14-hour pilgrimage from Seattle to Sundance with semi-regularity. Though I promise myself a chance to get a little work done in the passenger seat, it's a promise I never really intend to keep. I should have been a long-haul truck driver. I've always been a little jealous of their open highways brimming with a galaxy of possibilities. The road, snaking up distant mountain passes, was made for man to conquer. And even though I know millions have gone before me, road trips always somehow feel like I'm heading out West to a great, unknown and untamed land. If sitting behind the wheel on a long road trip somehow brings me closer to the part of me that wishes I was Lewis or Clark, then riding in the passenger seat is like watching a rerun documentary of the Lewis and Clark expedition. It just ain't the same.

The Red Cross medic warned me to avoid driving and "unnecessary thinking," whatever that means. Cognitive activity after a concussion can increase recovery time and the risk of permanent damage. But that didn't scare me. Not as much as spending the next fourteen hours with nothing to do but watch an old rerun of a documentary on Manifest Destiny. So I consoled myself by turning the passenger-seat-prison-sentence into an opportunity to start that novel I'd been putting off. And that's how Evan Burl was born. Yes, I started my first novel somewhere in the Rocky Mountains while I was following doctor's orders to avoid driving and "unnecessary thinking." So if you think *Evan Burl and the Falling* sucks, or if during disconcerting stretches of prose you begin to question my sanity, please remember that I was concussed when I began and therefore have a good excuse.

That road trip was nearly four years ago. Since then, dozens of versions of the novel have been splattered all over the web and hundreds of the most wonderful people in the world have spent countless hours sifting through pages of utter rubbish to provide feedback instrumental to its growth. It's been said that most authors write ten books before one of them escapes into the court of public opinion where well-meaning writers are drawn and quartered for offenses such as cliffhanger endings. I took a different route, opting to write the same book ten times. Well, more like a hundred. Through those thousands of hours and millions of words, I changed in a way that surprised me. I figured I would become a better writer with practice (gag-inducing glimpses at early drafts confirm that this indeed was the case), but I learned more than that. I learned to write for myself.

It seems like all the cool writers, the kind who wear ridiculously oversized glasses that they somehow pull off and dark turtlenecks and knit scarfs, they all have this whole writing for oneself thing down. They ooze big tears of authenticity out of their pores. I have disgusting friends like this, people who have been writing for years and have hard drives full of provoking prose (actually, the really cool writers do it longhand in black Moleskines), friends who have little intention of ever sharing their work with anyone. This is either an incredibly noble gesture or they're scared. Either way, they make me feel like a big commercial, compliment-fishing whore. The truth is I kind of was when I started. Somewhere along the way that changed. I think it was the feedback that did it, the good, the bad and the indifferent. The multiple two star reviews on the same day and the kindhearted emails I'd get from readers with variations on, "Dear God, please stop rewriting this book" and the people who went to creative lengths to tell me what an ugly little baby I'd conceived. Eventually, I learned not to care. Then I learned to do whatever I damn well pleased. Finally I learned to do what I loved. Now I believe the closer I get to this—I still have a bit of the old commercial whore to kill off —the better and more true my writing becomes.

I'm tempted to apologize for the changes, for the multi-year drawn out process that I've asked my readers again and again and again to endure with me, but that wouldn't be honest. Because I'm not sorry, in the best possible sense. I'm thankful. I don't think it matters how you get there. It might take a concussion or misplaced motivations or writing ten books before sharing one of them, or writing the same book a hundred times and releasing all of them on the internet for public bashing. The best writing plumbs the deep and unsearchable human heart, reflecting something about ourselves in a way that makes us strive to become more. You can't get to plumbing if you're fishing for compliments. At least, I've discovered, I can't.

So I guess I'm glad I took that last ski run. If I hadn't knocked my head, Evan Burl and his mentally unstable friends might forever have been locked up inside my own unstable brain. And I wouldn't have discovered my cathartic love for writing or developed the guts to write what I wanted without pandering to public opinion. The point is, great helpeters, like great artists, aren't out to win popularity contests. They do what they love because they love what they do. They keep their motives pure. These things are intangible, but they make a big difference when it comes to either being pretty good at something or great at it. Your audience can tell if you don't love what you do and if you're doing it to get money or something else from them.

APPLICATION FOR TODAY

How can you become more genuine with your helpeting? In what ways have you succumbed to the temptation to do what you do simply because it's a job or it needs to be done or you hope to get something from it? How can you change what you're doing to increase your connection to helping people for the right reasons? Try to make at least one tangible change to your approach to help you grow in this area.

PART 3.
MAKE IT EASY
FOR
CUSTOMERS
TO
UNDERSTAND
AND BUY YOU

BEING A PEOPLE PERSON ISN'T ENOUGH

When you live in Seattle, a place known worldwide for its rain and depressed, indie rock culture, flying to Orange County, California can make you feel like a million bucks. It started with tiny drops of rain pelting the window next to where I sat in 6A. My chariot turned down the runway, the jets fired, I was sucked back into my seat for a few minutes and then I was above the clouds where it's sunny 365 days a year. Two hours and thirty minutes later, I touched down at John Wayne Airport, where it's sunny nearly as often as in the upper half the troposphere.

A few minutes later, I took the keys to my convertible Ford Mustang and pulled out on palm tree lined MacArthur Blvd., on my way to see a man known by many as a master networker. We'll call him Stanton. I'd known Stanton for several years and was looking forward to sharing a Kuba Kuba cigar and a glass of his favorite Zinfandel on his gorgeous back porch a few short miles from the Pacific Ocean.

Stanton loves people. The first time we met, he insisted I stay in one of his three master bedroom suites, and he still insists whenever I travel anywhere in Southern California. It's like his house was built to be a hotel for traveling business people. When I stay at Stanton's, it's not uncommon for others to be staying, too. I've met Alabama fans, pastors, software executives and conference junkies on Stanton's back porch, where sweet cigar smoke seems to flow as endlessly as steam from a natural hot spring.

This particular trip, I was dropping in to attend a conference of about 800 leaders, a conference

Stanton is involved with running. A small circle of niche consultants often speak at Stanton's conference. They also do quite a bit of business with each other and often — at a particular outdoor Carlsbad karaoke bar that shall not be named — get quite a bit of business done after the conference is over. On this particular evening, after a few hours of trying to get Stanton to sing Desperado, I retired with him to his back porch where we watched birds dart back and forth across the fading sky.

"I don't get it," Stanton said.

I puffed my Kuba Kuba.

"All those guys come to this conference," he continued, "getting more business done in two days than I get done all year. And it's my conference!"

Stanton was a master of building relationships. By some measures he would have a prodigious volume of social capital. But he wasn't profiting from his relationships like the other business people who spoke at his conference. Stanton is an example of how one can possess relationships, even genius-level people skills, and yet not experience a measurable return on those skills.

Helpeting isn't just about helping people.

In fact, like Stanton, you can help millions of people and not get an ounce of financial benefit. In order to close the loop between helping people, building trust over time and seeing your business benefit, you must make it easy for your target customers to understand what you do and then buy it. It's easy to forget the need for this, and most helpeters do. For people to whom helping comes naturally, it's easy to miss the point that you must also keep your solution top of mind for your customers. And for these natural helpers, this is particularly hard to understand. How, helpful people wonder, can others whom I have trusting long-term relationships with not know what I do or how to buy what I'm selling? As we discussed before, your own mother will be confused about what you do if you can't communicate it clearly. And if your mom doesn't know what you do or if she could use your services, no one else will either. It's your job to make it easy for people to know what you do and how to buy. No one else is going to do this for you. This section explores this third step of profiting from helpeting.

LISTENING

Making yourself easy to buy and understand starts with listening. Get feedback from the people who are already doing business with you, whether you have a personal email list, a large database or a tight network. It's amazing how many companies try to create marketing strategies without getting feedback from their clients first. Why did your customers start buying your product or service in the first place? Why are they going to your church instead of the one closer to them? Or supporting your nonprofit instead of the one their brother works at? What value do your clients get out of a relationship with you? You have to be willing to ask the hard questions if you're going to gain much of value from listening. Questions like, do your customers like your products? Do they think your customer service stinks? How do they think you compare with your competitors? You might think they like you because of your products, but maybe they buy because you're the cheapest.

Get to know your customers.

How does an interaction with your organization feel? Are there aspects of your product your customers would love to change? How did they first hear about you? Was it a personal referral? Or do they simply drive past your business every day on the way to work? These are invaluable insights that will help you focus your marketing budget. If you're not already gathering answers to these questions, getting started is probably cheaper and easier than you think. There are numerous free or low cost solutions available today from AWeber email blasting to SurveyMonkey. Create a survey, post it on Twitter or Facebook, ask some questions and start listening.

APPLICATION FOR TODAY

Create a short survey using SurveyMonkey and ask your blog and social media audiences to fill it out. Ask questions about why people like your services or what drew them to you in the first place. If you're an individual, you can ask your friends and family to give input on what your best professional traits are and where you should focus your energies. Send out personal invites to clients or friends and request that they help you by filling out your survey. Then go over the results and use that information to hone your targeting pitch.

USING STORY TO MAKE YOUR MESSAGE STICK

When I arrived at Umpqua Bank in downtown Bellevue, Washington I was ushered through a door that said Employees Only and down a short hall to a corner office. Inside, ten business leaders sat around a table laughing, handing out business cards and catching up. Since I was the last to arrive, we began shortly after I found my seat. For a half hour, we each described our work to the group, giving an elevator pitch for what makes us unique and the kinds of people we do business with. This group exists for cultivating a referral network and if you haven't been to a meeting like this, you may not realize how common it is. These meetings are happening in boardrooms, coffee shops and small town city halls around the country every day.

After the initial introductions were complete, a man in his mid-fifties named Will, who specializes in fractional CFO work, went into his spotlight presentation. Usually—if I can be honest with you— these presentations are pretty dry. Well-meaning presenters often break many of the ten commandments of public speaking such as cramming too many excel spreadsheets on a slide, reading from notes or saying um more often than I get passed on the freeway when my dad is driving. But this presentation was different. Will started by telling a story. He told us about his childhood, how his father owned and operated a dairy farm that made the best ice cream for a hundred miles. How his dad worked seven days a week, taking no more than an hour for dinner before returning to work each evening. Will didn't resent his father taking so much time for his business. He recognized, then and now, that running your own business can run you. Will's father didn't know there was any other way.

During this story, Will didn't use any slides or notes and he never once said um. He seemed at ease and confident, though I don't think it was because he'd practiced twenty times in front of the mirror that morning. I think it was because he was telling his own story. I looked around the room at one point and noticed that not a single person was checking their phone. Many were leaning forward. They interrupted Will with questions. They laughed at his jokes. And when Will said that his dream is to help leaders get into the driver's seat of their businesses rather than being run over by them, everyone believed him. This all happened a few days ago and I can't remember any of Will's other points. But I have a feeling I'm going to remember Will's story for a long time. I can picture him as a child, wishing his father was around to play ball. And I can feel Will's passion for helping today's business leaders avoid the fate of his father.

The best networkers

are remembered by their colleagues when a need arises.

If someone asks you for a real estate agent, which one do you refer? You might find you actually know ten, but only one or two come to mind in the moment. Will did a fantastic job making himself memorable, and he's far more likely to come to my mind now when I hear about a business that might need his services. The same is true in many contexts of leadership, influence and life. If we become better storytellers, we're going to be more memorable, increase our influence and help more people grow.

APPLICATION FOR TODAY

What are your best stories that highlight your expertise? Have you practiced them? Try writing them down. Think of some interesting details that will make your stories more memorable. Find opportunities to work these stories into your customer meetings.

THE ESSENCE OF STORY

Story is a powerful tool for communicating who you are, why people should care and how they can engage with you. It's important to understand the elements of story in light of helping you hone your own fairytale, where you're the hero.

I thought I was being original when I picked storytelling as the topic for one of my first breakout sessions at a marketing conference. I ran into one of the keynote speakers in the greenroom, an author well-known for his ability to take dry subjects and make them engaging through story. When he asked what my breakout topic was, I proudly gave my title.

"Your speaking about story?" he said. Something about the way he asked it took the shine off my hopes of impressing him.

I straightened my shoulders. "Yeah. I thought it would be cool to help marketers engage their audiences better through story."

As he turned to scan the room for someone more important he said, "Oh great, I wonder if anyone at this conference isn't speaking about story."

I grabbed a schedule and sure enough, most of the topics had something to do with storytelling. Titles like *What story does your website tell?* and *Sell with story!* and *Your clothes tell a story, are they telling the right one?* I began to realize that story had been hijacked.

People aren't marketers anymore. They're storytellers. Today, everything must tell a story. Even if there is no story to tell. Your website must tell a story. Same for your packaging, office's ingress, fleet and, of course, the clothes you wear. The problem is, culture seems to be forgetting that stories weren't invented yesterday. Story is an actual thing that has been around for a really long time, as long as humans have roamed the fruited plain. Now I admit, it sounds a lot cooler to sell a story rather than just a plain old boring website. And websites can in fact tell a story, but many people who sell storytelling websites, wardrobes or marketing plans are telling stories themselves, with much exaggeration, and they're confusing a lot of people in the process.

SO WHAT IS STORY ANYWAY?

In order to answer that question, we have to understand where story came from. Stories were first told around fires. They were told by travelers, mothers, fathers, jesters, kings and fools. Uncles told stories about the elk that got away. Sisters tattled about brothers who pushed them in the river. Women told stories about how their husbands courted them. Men added details to those stories, noting how they'd loved their wives for two whole years before their wives would give them the time of day. Stories, at their most basic form, are a series of events. They're a plot. One could distill it down to a grocery list of events that are recounted in chronological order. But no mere series of events is going to be an engaging story in and of itself. Recounting my afternoon of meetings in painstaking detail isn't going to keep anyone's attention for more than about 10 seconds. Good stories, the ones worth telling, all have one thing in common: change.

In every story, someone changes. Sure circumstances change too, but it's the people in the stories we're most concerned with. Humans are social creatures and we want to hear about other people, even if those people are robots, animals or plants with human traits. Stories are about people changing. That's why stories were so important in the earlier years of our civilization, and why they remain important to this day. Stories are how we warn each other. They're how we raise our children. They're how we convince each other to do something, such as buying a stereo. They're how we inspire each other to stretch ourselves to reach our potential. This element is what's often missing from what people call stories. Too many think telling stories is simply recounting what happened, how they got here. But effective stories are centered on change. When you're selling something, what you're selling usually plays a central role in that change, i.e. your client's business was falling apart until they hired your consulting firm and now everything has changed for them.

Stories are infinitely more easy to remember than factoids.

Just think back to history class. Do you remember all the critical dates of the Civil War? Not likely. But I bet you remember the stories. You might even be able to picture movies you've seen about the war or recall the books you've read. You think about the people, even if you can't remember their names. You think about what was at stake and the lives that were changed. Most companies sell facts and features. Great companies sell stories. Great companies also use elements of story to improve their connection to customers. For example, most clothing companies show ads of beautiful people in beautiful locations with other beautiful people having fun or just looking cool. This is a form of scene setting and they're inviting the audience or target market to insert themselves into the scene. It's a sort of interactive storytelling element that allows the audience to enter into the story. And it only costs $119 for the dress that will take you there. This isn't a story, but it's an element of a story. And it allows you to imagine the life transformation you'll experience by purchasing the clothes and entering into the story the company is telling.

You can use this kind of lifestyle scene setting to your benefit, but it tends to be the method used by big budget advertisers. A more cost effective use of storytelling is simply recounting how a customer engaged with you and how their business was transformed. The beauty of this kind of storytelling is you don't even need to advertise your company. In fact, you should diminish your role as much as possible. Make the star of the story your customer. Your target market will connect the dots on their own and realize that you played an important role in that transformation.

Good stories are easy to remember and share.

When they feature what you do, how you do it and how a client is able to purchase it, it makes it easier for your target market to remember what you do and how they can access it for themselves. Keep telling these stories over and over every chance you get and over time people will actually start to remember what you said. It still takes awhile, but it will happen a lot faster than if you just spam people with boring facts about your company. The attraction to selling stories instead of whatever else people are hawking these days is that great storytelling has always been and will always be in demand. There is no technology, no industry change, no outsourcing opportunity, no economic downturn that will replace or reduce the need for story. The business model, the distribution system, the method of payment may change a million times, but a great storyteller will always have a place at the fire.

APPLICATION FOR TODAY

Begin to compile a list of stories that highlight your unique contribution to the world. Individuals can recount stories about how they helped their previous employers. Businesses can compile stories from customers about the change they experienced from working with them. Stories are the most valuable sales tool you have. You should plan to spend a considerable amount of time and money finding and developing your best stories. Great stories aren't just spit out the first time you think of them. You should have great storytellers on staff or retainer to help you craft those raw stories into something that's going to make you shine. And if you do this right, whatever you spend should be returned to you more than a hundredfold.

THE EXAMPLE OF CHARITY WATER

Charity Water is a great example of communications clarity. It doesn't take long to figure out what they do, how you can get involved, how you can give, what you get for your gift, why that's important and how many other people are getting involved. If every nonprofit communicated as clearly and effectively as Charity Water, I think the world's problems would probably be solved. Imagine the potential of applying this clarity to your personal brand or the brand of your company.

One of the biggest problems nonprofits face is they become blind to their own shortcomings. How can they help it? They're in the trenches doing the work every day and it's hard to detach yourself from that when it's time to market your cause to donors. Yet the most successful nonprofits all have one thing in common: their public message is crystal clear. They might do a billion different things behind the scenes but publicly they're all about one thing and one thing only. Usually that one thing is easy to get involved with while what you get is clear and powerfully reinforced with stories. I've consulted with nonprofits who struggle to narrow their focus publicly. They can't let go of all the great things they do or narrow down their mission to one thing, but people get confused when you tell them the fourteen things you do well. Their attention spans are about as long as a hair is wide. So when you say you do fourteen things they might think it's really great, but their reaction is to run. They run to another nonprofit that only does one thing really well, at least as far as they can tell from the outside. They can understand that one thing and they can get involved easily. For-profit business is the same way. The vast majority of the best businesses, ones that far outperform their peers, do one thing and they do it well—at least as far as their public, spearhead of communication is concerned.

A company can do many things behind the scenes. They just need to slowly introduce those things to their

customers over time.

You can't let loose with the fire hose all at once. You have to spoon feed your customers. "I see you bought this from us, did you know we can do that for you, too?" Slowly, you occupy a greater and greater portion of your customer's lives, but never lose sight of your crystal, outward clarity. Even the customers who have given over 51% of their lives to a single company have it easier with a company that's clear about their one thing. This is because it's easier for this great customer to become an evangelist for that company's cause. They can't very well tell their friends about the fourteen things some organization does. They need just one thing to recommend, and one thing only. Otherwise they get confused about how to introduce you and when people are confused, it's too much work and they just don't follow up.

Now you might be thinking, "What about General Electric? They do thirty thousand things. Or what about CocaCola? They own restaurant chains and chips and even water brands." First, both of these examples are huge companies. Huge companies don't count. Why? For one thing, this book isn't written for people who are running 100 billion dollar companies. For another, those companies play by different rules and there are only a small number of them anyway. They're so big entire books have been written about their ways. And most of the stuff in those books isn't all that helpful because if you're not also running a huge conglomerate, you can't really apply it. I'll always remember a Q&A with a big time CEO. He was asked how he handles changes to the marketing space as it relates to social media. The CEO answered, "We have a consulting firm on a million dollar retainer to deal with that stuff, otherwise I don't know how I would manage it." Needless to say, the guy sitting next to me, the owner of a company with six employees, didn't find the CEO's answer all that helpful. Also, each of the large conglomerates still follows the principles of clarity, even if they do so in a different way. It may be that each of their divisions needs to be crystal clear about their one thing, and maybe the divisions within those divisions need to do this. In the end, the principles are the same for large companies as they are for small companies. People need clarity to understand what someone can do for them. In fact, it has been my experience that the larger and more complicated a company, the better they are at communicating clearly what they do. That's because they likely wouldn't have gotten so big if they didn't figure that out somewhere along the way. Just look at Walmart. Their slogan is Better Living. They sell a million things in thousands of warehouses around the world and they've narrowed down what they do to two words. Compassion International is a billion dollar nonprofit that does enormous work around the world, but publicly they are known as being the place to go if you want to sponsor a child for thirty-eight bucks a month. You can do a lot of things, you just can't lead with them all publicly.

APPLICATION FOR TODAY

List the things you do for your customers or employers. How can you narrow that list down to one thing and make that your public spearhead? This can't usually be done in a day, but the journey should begin today. Give it a try and then test out your message publicly. You might find that over the course of a couple years you'll continue to tweak and hone your message until you find something that really grabs people.

CLARITY PLUS EASY

The issue of clarity goes even further than we discussed in the last chapter. Clearly, helping people will get you nowhere if they don't understand what you do and how to buy it. You need to put in the legwork to understand your unique place in the world so that when you're given that great opportunity to pitch what you do to the VP of your perfect client, you can take full advantage. If you don't have your value down in that moment, you're likely going to lose out on doing business with that client. You can't keep your value top of mind for clients and prospects if you don't know what it is yourself. This is essential to making yourself easy to understand and buy, because there's really a third component at work here: making yourself easy to refer. People won't ever refer something they don't understand.

The more you understand your value, the more clearly and often you'll communicate it.

When you repeat it again and again, people will begin to remember. It takes a frustratingly long time for people to remember, but they will. The truth is, we can't blame them for not remembering what we do if we don't know what it is that we do. They have their own lives to worry about, we can't expect them to do our job for us. So before you waste another opportunity to make yourself easy to understand and buy, take the time to write down your unique offering. Memorize it. Say it in your sleep. It's going to take time, but the more you practice the more it will become a part of you. And the best part is you can begin wherever you are. Communicate your value in the clearest, shortest possible way whenever you get the chance. Try different approaches. Change it up. Get coaching. Ask others for input. Hone your message. Over time, it will become clear. But it doesn't happen by accident, at least not for most people. It happens if you work hard at it for a long time.

APPLICATION FOR TODAY

Imagine you step into an elevator and right before the door closes the CEO of a company that you're dying to win as a client steps in next to you. She hits the 40th floor button and you feel the floor rise up under you. The CEO turns to you, and recognizing you from a social event, asks "Remind me what you do again?" You now have 30 seconds to sell her on your awesomeness and, hopefully, be invited off the elevator with her when you reach the 40th floor to discuss how you can help her company more. This is called the 30 second elevator pitch. Try writing down your own version of this pitch. Then try it on as many people as you can. If they're friends or they know your business well, ask them for feedback. When you get a good 30 second pitch, try to distill your value down to a few words. BMW is the ultimate driving machine. Starbucks is your third place. Disneyland is the happiest place on earth. These are billion dollar brands and decades of messaging practice, but they are the high bar we should all strive for when it comes to clarity and power.

THE YOU GAP

There's a you-sized gap in this world that only you can fill. Every person or organization needs to discover and develop what makes them unique. Consider what that is for you or your business and how you can develop your ability to help others by owning who you are. I've both avoided and embraced my own quirks and I can say from personal experience, it can be a rough road.

I was about twelve years old when I realized something at the core of my being: I was a nerd. Not just any nerd. If there was such a thing as a nerd king, I would have slain that kid in a leadership coup and laughed as I sat on his throne. I suppose it was my misguided assumption that girls would not want to hang around the King of the Nerds. So in my formative years, I made a decision. I was going to be popular, and not just any popular. I was going to go from the biggest nerd at my school to the coolest guy in my zip code. It couldn't be that hard right? So began a multi-decade journey, a moderately successful one, of trying to be someone I was not. I determined that not only was I going to be well-liked, I was going to be rich. Over more than 15 years, I tried my hand at a few different careers. I've been paid to be an electrician, songwriter, gardener, plumber, videographer, photographer, fabricator, welder, contractor, developer, graphic designer, web designer, house framer, narrator, illustrator—you get the idea. This list goes on. And on and on. I was trying to discover what I was good at. Never once did it occur to me that there might be a string that ran through all these changes. The signs were there, though.

All through school, whatever teacher I had would encourage me to explore a career in the field they taught. The science teacher thought I had a talent for science. The English teacher thought I should become a writer. The PE teacher thought—well scratch that. I wasn't ever any good at PE. I was frustrated by their responses. I had ten different people telling me to do ten different things with my life. Looking back, I can see what they were really telling me was that I was good at learning. This same skill enabled me to do about three hundred different careers—maybe not brilliantly, but well enough to provide for my family. I picked up a variety of skills well enough to get by for a while, but they never quite fit. I grew tired of whatever I was doing as soon as I'd learned about 70% of what it might take to reach mastery—a point where I reached a level of diminishing return on my investment of energy.

Here's the key point. I was blind to the idea that loving change might actually be an asset. As far as I was concerned, working the same job for twenty years was the kind of thing people had to do in hell, but it was what you were supposed to do. It was what all the guys around me who actually did something with their life did and I was desperately trying to find my piece of that 20 year pie. All the while, I never stopped to honestly ask myself, "What am I made to be?"

I still can't say that I've found the answer to that question. I may not know for sure until my time here on Earth is done, but I'm a lot closer today than I was then. It seems so obvious looking back. The evidence has been knocking me on the noggin since I was in pre-school, but it wasn't until I let go of my agenda, giving up my desires for wealth, fame and success, that I was able to see the string that ran through all of my different careers. I'm happier now, more fulfilled in my work, even more focused, but that's a side effect. The truth is, by discovering more about my own uniqueness, I was able to narrow my drive and my desire for change in a way that proved helpful to other people.

I realize this is a very personal story and I hesitated to share it because this book isn't about me. It's about you. But I want you to know where I'm coming from and that perhaps there's someone else who has experienced some of the same frustrations that you might have had in your quest to find your place in this world. Your details will be different than mine, but I bet there are some things you want that might be blinding you from seeing what you were made to be.

There are no ordinary people.

Every person who ever breathed fresh air — and even those who never breathed — were unique from the moment of conception. It's not a matter of choice. We don't choose to be unique. We just are. Our choice lies in what we do with it. Will we embrace who we are? Most of us don't. Most of us try to be someone else. But to help those around us, we must embrace who we are. We must develop our uniqueness and share our uncommon self with the world.

Some of us were made with low energy. Some, with high. Some of us were made for taking risk. Some, for safety. Some of us were made to lead masses of people. Some, to lead a few.

It's culture that judges which of these traits is more worthy of praise than others. But since when was culture worth listening to? Listen to yourself. What were you made to be? Be that. Be the best version of that you can be. Trying to be someone we are not is mentally sapping. It's horrible to wake up Monday morning and drive in to a job that isn't meant for you. What if we could find our place? What if we were excited to get up on Mondays? I believe it's possible. I believe you can. You do it by being yourself.

WALT DISNEY

Born in 1901, Walt Disney loved to draw cartoons and write comics as a child. He dreamed of making people happy and he believed in this dream so much that he was constantly running into opposition. Every major step forward that Walt made was met with resistance from every direction. His brother and business partner, his wife, his friends, his employees and, of course, the press were always against his dreams, even as they watched him succeed. Walt was told he would sink the company so many times that he was shocked when, during the filming of *Mary Poppins*, everyone went along without a fight. He joked, "I wonder if they're finally accepting that I might know what I'm doing."

Of course, Walt did almost sink his company multiple times. And there were always people waiting to swoop in and take away what he had built. When Walt was in his early twenties with a successful business, he went to New York City to close a deal with a distribution partner. Instead of getting the deal done, Walt learned that this partner was stealing his entire company, with the staff and creative content. Most of us might give up after that, find a "normal" job, do something more steady. Not Walt. On the train ride home, he created Mickey Mouse, one of the most iconic cartoons ever dreamed up. That's how unique people often react to failure or opposition. They use it as an opportunity for something better. Something else that was unique about Walt was his presence. He had time for the things we wouldn't normally expect an important and busy CEO to attend to. One time, when the prototypes of the cars at Autotopia were being designed, an engineer called to see when Walt could come see the progress. Walt, rather than setting up an appointment, hopped in his car and drove across LA that moment to see how it was coming. Walt was always available for the small details. He even did some of the painting to help Disneyland open on time.

Walt died relatively young, but his legacy lives on today and will for many years to come because Walt chose to be himself. Despite the opposition, he offered the world what only he could offer. How tragic would it have been had Walt decided to be a good boy and get in step with the rest of the world? We, too, can build a legacy and make the difference we were designed to make, even while other people laugh in our face.

Everyone is unique.

There is no recipe for uniqueness. It's not a commodity to be bought and sold and it doesn't come with step-by-step directions. It's like a song. Or a novel. Or a great plate of coconut shrimp with orange marmalade. The length of time and the steps it will take you to realize your own unique role is going to vary. Each person has their own path, a unique journey to a unique destination. That said, just as with art and great cooking, there are some general rules, guidelines to help us find our way.

First, everyone is unique. But some people are more unique than others. This isn't necessarily a happy fact, but it's a fact nonetheless and we can take it in one of two ways. One, we can fret about it, throw a fit, give up, yell obscenities and cry at our own party. Or, we can accept this fact of life as the freeing reality it is: we can't become someone we're not and we shouldn't expect to. I believe the real lesson here is to worry less about how unique we are and instead just try to be the best version of ourselves we can be. Everyone can do that. And besides, if everyone had the same magnitude of uniqueness, that wouldn't be very unique.

The second rule of finding what makes you uncommon is that jealousy, laziness, pride, ignorance and bitterness are your enemies. There are other negative traits equally detrimental, but you get the idea. You're never going to find what makes you special if you're consumed with what makes your neighbor special. It's difficult to discover your uniqueness if you prefer to lie in bed and watch TV. If you think you're pretty amazing and the world just never seems to catch on, you're unlikely to get far in your quest for un-commonality. Bitterness, perhaps more than anything else, can derail your journey. If this is your tendency, I'd like to encourage you to step off that train. Forgive yourself. Forgive your parents or your friends or your spouse or whoever else has been holding you back. It's up to you to move forward and, in the end, you have no one to blame but yourself if you don't get where you want to go. How can I have the audacity to say that? Because there are lots of people who lived in their uncommon niche, serving and changing the world around them, who overcame great disadvantage. There are a lot of tragic happenings in this world and I don't intend to make light of them, but by holding onto bitterness you're letting those tragic circumstances beat you up again and again. You're letting them win. It's hard. *It is hard*. But you can rise above what's been done to you and where you've come from to become the person you were born to be.

Third, consider your childhood. Walt Disney doodled cartoons when he was supposed to be studying. His parents couldn't get him to stop drawing. Sometimes the hobbies you love as a child, the interests you have and the character ticks that make you odd all add up to be the same characteristics that make you unique as an adult. How were you unique as a kid? What were you obsessed with? If you're destined to become a great guitarist, it's likely you never forced yourself to practice as a kid. Yes, you practiced. You practiced a lot. But you didn't think of it as practice. It wasn't a chore. You're parents didn't have to remind you to do your scales. In fact, they could barely get you to stop playing that dang guitar long enough to eat dinner with the family. That's the way it is sometimes with the things that make us unique. While other people think of what we do as a chore, you can't get us to stop. This can often lead us to discover our unique place in this world. Often, but not always. It doesn't always work. Many people have a hard time remembering anything that fits this description. Maybe you were what you would describe as an average kid with average interests. That's okay and it means one of two things. Either it's your averageness that makes you unique or this tool for discovering what makes you uncommon isn't the right one for you. Don't worry. There are other tools to help you on your journey, just as there are other guidelines.

Finding your place in this world can take a lifetime.

Discovering your place in this world is not an overnight thing. My very unscientific research (asking random people I meet) indicates that many people don't figure out their life purpose until their mid to late forties. The problem we have is that magazines and newspapers are all filled with 30 most influential people under 30 lists and billionaire techies who can barely drive a car and bestselling authors who tried their hand at writing in English 101 and turned out a Hemingway. These are rare exceptions, not the rule. Banking on, or evaluating ourselves against these benchmarks is like investing our 401(K) in the Mega Millions jackpot. Sure, some people win, but it's not exactly a retirement plan.

It can't be for your own glory.

Why? Because being unique isn't about you. It's about others. And one can't be about others and about their own glory at the same time. It's the sharing of one's gifts and uncommon characteristics that closes the loop, provides the final link in the chain. Seeking your own glory from your uniqueness cuts that link and keeps the loop from closing. And that makes it a waste of time. We were made to serve others. Our uniqueness enables us to do it like no one else in the world. You can use your uniqueness for yourself, certainly, but I don't think you'll be maximizing your potential if you do.

If you think you're not unique, I'd be willing to bet that you're carrying some form of pre-conceived notion about uniqueness. Try to let go of what culture says is important. Start with a blank slate and build from there. If you still can't figure out where to start, you might consider hiring a personal coach or asking a trusted friend for help. Sometimes we just can't see ourselves clearly and need to enlist the help of others. You're not likely to peg it in your first try and, in reality, this is a lifelong journey of discovery. But the closer we can get to aligning what makes us unique with our daily activities, the more helpful we'll be to everyone around us and the more joy we'll find in the daily grind. The most important part is that you care enough about finding your uniqueness that you make a serious attempt to try.

APPLICATION FOR TODAY

Spend some time thinking about what makes you unique in this world. This might take 30 minutes, or it could take a weekend. Try writing down a few statements we normally associate with businesses such as a mission statement, a unique value proposition or a 30 second pitch. What is the perfect day like for you? How can you have that day and help people at the same time? These are just a few ways to begin to unravel how you fit into this giant puzzle.

THE INFINITE POWER OF SAMPLES

Placerville is a quaint, wealthy town halfway between Sacramento and Reno. It seems to be quite literally cut from the mountains with huge cliff faces rising up on all sides. Each Saturday morning, white tents rise from a parking lot and a couple dozen vendors unload hand knit baby clothes and wood-fired pizza ovens and coffee carafes to sell to the hundreds of middle age former yuppies who have escaped San Francisco to live in the mountains. For a summer I left each Friday at midnight to drive my four door, long bed GMC pickup full of boxes from a sausage processor outside Eugene, Oregon down I-5 so I could join the other vendors. It was an eight hour drive, as long as I averaged 80 and got my meals via drive through. I would arrive at 8 in the morning, set up my tent, sell something like $2,000 in sausages, pack up the leftovers a little after noon and drive home hopefully in time to tuck my kids into bed late Saturday night. Why would anyone expose themselves to this strange form of torture involving 16 plus hours of driving and 4 hours of selling at a farmers market each week for an entire summer? For one, the money was pretty good for a 23 year-old. Most of that $2,000 was margin and I kept whatever I made. Plus my partner, who was in charge of the farming, and I were selling our products into high-end restaurants and niche retail chains, places who are known to send their buyers and chefs to obscure markets like Placerville to find the most cutting edge and exciting new farmers. But my reasons are for another time. The point I want to get to is how I outsold every other vendor at the market. It all has to do with samples.

I would go through dozens of packages of our signature cooked sausage link, Louisiana hot links, cajun bourbon and jalapeño flavored sticks of pure joy. I'd smile and look each person in the eye as they passed my booth with my outstretched hand offering a little something tasty to get them to slow down. And slow down they did. It's something about human nature and farmers market culture, but when you see a crowd outside a booth, you want to buy.

I'd get a few people stopping and eating my samples and before I knew it a crowd would be calling out orders. With one hand I'd be taking twenties and with the other I'd be handing out more samples. One pack of hot links for $10 or three for $20. I was sweating by the time noon rolled around. I've never been what anyone would describe as a great salesperson. I don't have a charismatic personality. I'm not a fast talker. I'm really an introvert. And yet I could act like an extrovert for four hours and hand out samples and it worked like magic. I learned the power of sampling that summer and I'll never forget.

Since then I've seen how many successful companies use sampling to gain customers. Most software companies have trials. Costco does really well with samples on Saturday mornings. Car companies are even allowing you to drive the car home for a night before you decide to buy. The more excitement we can build around our sampling programs and the more we can allow people to try out what we're offering, the more successful we'll become. This principle is true for individuals as much as it is for companies. Yet many individuals haven't figured this out.

A friend of mine, Gentry, was looking to hire a writer to help tell stories about the nonprofit work he was doing in Africa. His organization was growing and he had recently won the opportunity to write enough stories to bring someone on staff full-time. That job hadn't started yet and wouldn't for a couple of months. In the meantime, Gentry had a tiny little writing job that he could have easily done himself, but he wanted to use it as an opportunity to get to know a possible hire before bringing them on. He put up ads for a freelancer who would be willing to do a small job and let the applicants know that there was about 1,000 or more hours of work coming in the next month, if they were a good fit.

No one responded.

So Gentry went to his network and was able to get in touch with a few possible options. The first was a small agency that was really more of a one man freelance operation. This person was glad to do the work, but for $750. Gentry responded that this was about 15 minutes of work (he'd done plenty of similar tasks himself), a trial for the purpose of seeing how well a writer fit with the organization. The freelancer wasn't interested and insisted that the work would take 10 hours.

Gentry moved on to another connection that looked very promising. This person had recently lost their job and was looking for full-time work with benefits. Gentry said that he was willing to make that happen if they were a good fit. In the meantime, with the deadline pressing, Gentry asked this writer if he would be willing to do this small job as a favor. Gentry did need it done quickly, but he was also using this as a chance to see how the candidate responded. After several emails back and forth, Gentry discovered that the writer's quoted rate had gone up 40% since their first email and still Gentry agreed to pay the full rate for as much as two hours, whatever it took to get the job done right. So Gentry collected the information necessary to get this person set up for payment as a contractor and connected him with the project managers. A few days later, Gentry got an email from the writer, who informed him he would not be doing the job because he needed to focus on his job search. Gentry was astonished. Hadn't he made it clear a full-time position was available? Even if Gentry hadn't had a job opening, he knew several other people looking for good writers and could have easily set this guy up with interviews.

Now quite late delivering this small project to his client, Gentry attempted one last time with a new contractor. Though the particulars were different and this person was more respectful of Gentry's time, the third contractor also declined to complete the job. After a month of emails and searching, Gentry did the job himself in 15 minutes and was no closer to finding a full-time solution.

Now, I don't know if this experience is indicative of today's millennial generation or if it is reflective of a universal disconnect between helping people and receiving the benefits that can come from that mindset. Had any of these three contractors simply helped Gentry out, they would likely have received more work than they could handle, at their full rates and on their own terms. Gentry had even made it clear that if there was too much work, he'd hire more people. But not one of the three contractors was willing to do a small job, however slightly inconvenient it might have been. How often in life do you have the opportunity to get paid to go to an interview? More than that, these contractors missed a valuable opportunity to allow a potential client/employee to sample their services. Just as I found when I was selling sausages in Placerville, providing samples of whatever it is we want people to buy is a time tested method for increasing interest in one's products or services. Even if we can't smile on a sidewalk with a sausage platter in hand, we can find some way to make it easy for people to try before they buy. The more fun, easy, exciting and urgent we make it, the better. Is it possible to create a frenzy of customers around our samples, even if we're selling software? You bet it is. Recently thegrid.io sold more than 15,000 new subscribers before their website building tool was even released. The Grid's primary product, for which over 15,000 people paid an entire year in advance, wasn't even previewed. All they had was a sexy video, peer pressure, excellent use of crowd funding, social media and enough of a peek at the product to create buyer interest. That's what sampling is really about. Creating buyer interest. This can be done by letting someone drive a car before they purchase or by showing just enough to grab an audience's attention. The better the attention grabbing, the greater the frenzy. This is the same process used by movies to get people in the seats. Before huge numbers of critical reviews were available to the average ticket buyer in one place, audiences relied on the previews, and maybe a favorite critic or two, to decide if they wanted to see a movie or not. They got a sample.

The thing about samples: they better be good.

They're your best chance to grab someone or push them away. If my partner in farming had been terrible at picking recipes and our sausages tasted like cardboard, I wouldn't have sold any sausages no matter how many samples I gave out. Be honest with yourself. If your samples stink, you had better go to the product team or your manager or the drawing board and get that straight. Or maybe just go find someone else to work for. If you can't rely on your samples to be good, you're not going to do well. Same thing for selling your own skills to an employer. If you offer to do a free marketing plan for your potential boss and she discovers through the process that you can't spell, you don't know the difference between social media and socialism and you devote 80% of your budget to newspaper advertisements, you're probably not going to get the job. Your samples have to knock it out of the park. In fact, if you think of your sampling as a job interview or a stage performance, you'll do better at ensuring your performance warrants an encore.

APPLICATION FOR TODAY

How can you make it easier for customers to sample what you sell? Make a plan to improve the quality and quantity of your sampling. Go over the top in what you allow customers to experience for free without any commitment. If they like what you offer, you can't give too much of it away for free (unless you're selling funeral services). They'll come back for more, and they'll be happy to pay your full price if they love it.

SHOW AND TELL

People who get tons of referrals are easy to refer. The best way to be easy to refer is to have something to bring to show and tell. You remember show and tell from first grade, right? Everybody brought something from home that they were proud of and showed it off to the class. We need to reinstitute show and tell as adults. We should have something we're proud of to show off and give away. Even better, we should give a pile of these to our referral partners so when they're wandering the great wide world, they have something to give to a potential customer when our name comes up.

The best handout is a book.

Nothing says you've got your act together like having your very own book. Nothing makes for a better referral than when a need comes up in a conversation and one of your referral partners reaches into their briefcase and pulls out your book, a book that explains exactly what to do to solve the problem they were just discussing. If that person really does have a problem, and if your referral partner has any trust with them, you can be almost certain they're going to at least flip through your book. If you've done a good job and your book is well written, full of good advice, has a professional cover and looks like it's been published by a company that knows what it's doing, then why wouldn't that person call you? Then, when they call you and set an appointment with your assistant, they're going to feel like they're meeting their hero when you walk up and shake their hand. You'll seem famous to them. We can't help but bestow that same sort of magic intangible power that we give to famous people to someone whose books we've read and appreciated. That's the power of having a great item to share with people, something you've made sure to do right, and giving lots of copies to anyone you think might run into one of your potential customers.

A few other handouts will help you fill out your referral arsenal.

A simple but attractive card, business size or otherwise, that offers something helpful along with your contact information is one option. A well designed, letter size page that describes your unique value (referred to as a one sheet). A magazine with an article you wrote. We're not talking about crappy car shaped magnets and hokey calendars with pictures of waterfalls. Not that you can't create swag that people want (and if you do create swag, make sure it's extraordinary or you'll be spending your free time pulling it out of trash cans and picking it up in the parking lot), but create something simple, clear and, ideally, valuable.

Along these lines, create a small card that describes your perfect prospect. This should include their profile, clues that indicate they'd be a good lead, questions that will help to determine if they'd be a good introduction and how best to introduce you. You might even put your 30 second value pitch on this card to make it easy for your referral partners to pitch you. Remember, the easier you make it to refer you, the more referrals you'll get. Even very well intentioned people are too busy with their own lives to take the initiative on figuring out how to tell others about you. Give these cards to whomever you think will take referring you seriously. More importantly, make sure you understand each person you give one of those cards to just as well as you want to be understood. If they don't have a referral card to give you, write down all their information where you can find it and keep it top of mind so you can be an even better referral source to them than you hope they'll be to you.

APPLICATION FOR TODAY

Come up with the best show and tell item you can muster in the next 24 hours and make it happen. For your first one, you might write a short essay filled with valuable insights and put your value proposition and contact information at the bottom. In time you can develop something more sophisticated, eventually a full-fledged book in all its splendor. Don't wait for that to get started on this. It's too important and having something clear and well done but simple is far better than nothing. Print off your item on quality paper and start giving stacks to people you think might refer you. Encourage them to do the same back to you.

PRESENTATION COUNTS

In the movie *Clueless* the main character, Cher, has decided to adopt a hopelessly out of fashion transfer from another school named Tai as her makeover project. As they're walking into school, Cher bestows some choice wisdom on her new friend. "You have something going for you that no one else in this school does. You could have been the most popular girl in your school." The lesson: when people don't know your background, you can present yourself in such a way as to move to a new social setting, from loser to the most popular girl in school. This lesson can be applied in a lot of areas of life. Some people call it fake it till you make it. Others call it putting your best foot forward. Still others call it perception is reality. No matter what you call it, it works.

When you meet someone for the first time, they're working off a very limited amount of information about you.

They might have looked you up on LinkedIn, read your bio on a website or received a little information about you from whoever referred them to meet with you. All in all, that's not a lot to go on when we're talking about the fact that each of us has potentially decades of life and experience and background. When you set up the appointment they get a little more information, like how you talk, the signature on your email or whether you set your own appointments or have an assistant do that. As soon as they set their eyes on you, they begin to accumulate more and more information. How you dress, how you hold yourself, how much time you spend on your hair each morning. As you sit with them at the coffee table, they get an avalanche of data: if you're comfortable talking with them, if you're confident, intelligent, arrogant, if you care about them, if you're likable. By the time you get to the point of making any kind of proposal or officially applying for a job or whatever it is, they have what they feel is a pretty complete picture of who you are. Of course the reality is that they can only possibly know a tiny fraction of who you are. It would take years to know you really well, if you could even be known well in that amount of time. Yet they're going to make a decision that affects your future based on what they've seen of you so far and the best news is that you have control over most of what they know. You can affect what people say about you, at least in the long-term, by managing your reputation well. You can have a good bio (written by someone else). You can manage your online presence. You can certainly manage how you dress, the things you talk about, how you hold yourself and every other aspect of the meetings you have with this person. Still, so many of us give little thought, care or planning to these perceptions, haphazardly throwing the opinion people have of us to the random winds.

It's very interesting to consider that when you sit down with

someone for the first time, they really don't know if you're a pauper or a billionaire.

They don't know if you're the #1 salesperson in your company or the guy who is about to be fired for missing his quota for the fourth straight month. They don't know if you can afford to pay your rent. They don't know if you're a loner or a high-functioning drunk or a psychopath. All they know is what you present. I'm not an advocate for presenting a lie. However, I am absolutely arguing that we should present the version of ourselves that we wish to become. If we want to become a billionaire, everything we do should reflect ourselves as if we already are. People will naturally start to assume that we're very successful and success will start to come more easily. If we want to be a highly sought public speaker who earns $50,000 an hour on a stage, then we should carry ourselves with the confidence that such a person would have. If we want to be the #1 salesperson, then we should act like a #1 salesperson. This can and should be done without going into crippling debt or lying. Not all billionaires drive expensive cars. Be the kind of billionaire who drives a Honda, if that's what you have in your driveway. You can update your wardrobe at high-end second hand stores and no one knows if you wore that sports coat yesterday, not if they're meeting you for the first time.

Just don't lie. Never lie about who you are. Don't brag about deals that you didn't win or places you haven't been or achievements you didn't earn. This will haunt you and you'll become known as a horrible person. If you have no amazing accomplishments to brag about, you might use the space in which you would otherwise have been bragging to listen to the person across from you instead. Convey your success with the straightness of your shoulders, the comfortable smile you offer the cashier as they take your order, the firmness of your handshake, the openness of your posture and the engagement of your eyes. A commitment to truth doesn't mean that you bring up how your electricity was turned off the night before. It is fully honest and ethical to only present the positive side of yourself. In fact, by showing your desperation or revealing your negative traits you're engaging in attempted manipulation and/or self-limiting sabotage in order to ensure that you remain in your current state. This often results from fear, and if that's your issue you should seek an excellent coach to work you through it.

Perception really is reality. And the cool thing is, you can present any reality (within the bounds of truth) that you wish. Why not present the reality that you hope to become and watch how your presentation helps you reach the goals you've set? How does this have anything to do with helpeting? You can't help people if you don't have their respect. Earn their respect and your influence will grow, enabling you to increase your helpfulness.

APPLICATION FOR TODAY

Look candidly at yourself in the mirror (figuratively and literally). How are you presenting yourself? What messages are you sending? How can you align the messages you send with the ones you wish to send? Start tweaking your presentation today and make a commitment to take charge of how people perceive you.

FOLLOW-UP

One sign that you've been successful at helpeting is that you get requests to do speaking engagements. This is even better when you get paid, but even free events can become paid gigs if you're good at turning them into business. In fact, you can considerably up your "speaking fee" by landing business from your engagements. How does a helpeter get the most out of these opportunities? We're going to delve into that topic now.

Just because people enjoy your talk doesn't mean they'll engage with you ever again. Just like all other areas of helpeting, you have to make it easy for customers to buy you, even if in this case buying you is subscribing to your email list or following you on Twitter. But it's important to make sure that your talk isn't all about you. Actually, your talk should not be about you at all. It's all about the audience and serving them. Don't hold back your best ideas for your book or your paid consulting gigs. Public speaking is one of the best opportunities to serve a large number of people at once and you want to make sure that you serve them to the best of your ability by giving away your very best ideas. If you're going to maximize your ROI on the event, you'll want to make sure to really impress the audience with not only your quality content, but your willingness to selflessly share your intellectual property. The people in attendance did, after all, pay to be there even if they only paid with the gas and time it took out of their day.

Once you've taken care of the content portion of your talk, it's important to make engaging with you incredibly easy and fun and to try and build a bit of urgency around it to ensure that human nature and laziness doesn't get the best of your audience. Perhaps the best way to do this is to have a custom landing page created just for the event. You could make it something like justinblaney.com/landingpage. Yes, this is a real landing page you can go check out to get an idea of how to make one. Your page must be well designed, reinforce your unique value, offer an incredible free resource and ask for something in order to access that resource. Ideally the resource you offer will directly relate to the talk you gave. I like to create a bundle of resources for this purpose. Something like the slides to the talk, my personal notes, a handout that will help the audience implement the ideas presented in the talk and, most importantly, my ebook that takes these ideas so much further and showcases stories and case studies to help. Give your resources a fair market value. The bundle I mentioned would be somewhere in the $199 range. That sounds like a fair price to get all that helpful insight. You might even put up some sample screenshots of what they'll be downloading. On the landing page you should have your picture and a photo of all those resources presented in a way that looks physical, not digital. If it's an ebook, it should look like a hardback book. This isn't false advertising, it just makes the book look more like a book. If it's an audio series or podcast, it should look like those old-fashioned audio books people bought that were on 10 CDs.

Resist the temptation to oversell your offer.

It's a little pitchy and annoying when you have these long pages that go on and on about the value. Just state what they get, put a dollar value on it and include a testimonial or two. Then make your ask. What do you most want to get from this person in exchange for this offer? It's best to just ask for their email address. I do this by asking, "Where do you want us to send the download?" Then I add that they'll receive free updates from my blog or something to that effect so they know they're subscribing to an ongoing list. I also note that I will not sell their information to anyone. Do this and follow through on that promise. Nothing is less helpful than getting spammed by someone's buddies.

If you've earned the right to ask for more than one thing by being incredibly helpful and having a package of goodies that is so enticing that you can get away with it, you can try to qualify the lead in some way. You could ask what position they're in at their company or for some other pieces of demographic info. You can also ask them to like you on Facebook or follow you on Twitter. There are simple plugins available that make this easy. I never ask for more than 2-3 things from someone, and if I ask for three I make all of them very easy to do.

They shouldn't have to leave the page to do anything or your results will be greatly diminished.

There are at least two possible ways to create some urgency around this free offer that will increase your results. One is to offer a giveaway to anyone who signs up within an hour of your talk. Make sure your landing page looks good on a phone because that's what everyone will be looking at it on while you're speaking. You might offer to give them the entire collection of your books, signed and delivered anywhere in the U.S. Or you could offer a $100 Amazon gift card. Or, if you have a larger budget, offer an iPad or Macbook. Yes, that's expensive, but if you're talking to a large audience and can manage to get 1,000 people to sign up for your list and like your Facebook page, you're only going to be paying a dollar per lead. That's a lot cheaper than almost any other way to get qualified leads who have already heard you establish your authority in an area that they might be interested in purchasing. The other way to build urgency is to limit the number of downloads. Something like half the audience. For example, if about 200 people are in attendance, limit the downloads to the first 100 that sign up. Don't worry about missing a few people. You're unlikely to get more than 50% of your audience signing up anyway. With every minute that passes after your talk ends, your chances of getting someone to sign up goes down exponentially. By the next morning they will likely have forgotten that you even exist. So you need to do everything you can to get them to sign up immediately.

Though your talk is all about your audience, you might feel that promoting your email list is about you and contrary to helpeting. That could be true depending on how you present it. If you bring up constantly how people can sign up for your email list during, before and after your talk, then no, you're not a helpeter. But if you, at the end of your talk, say something along the lines of, "I've attended a hundred talks just like this one, many of them probably quite a bit more interesting"—self-effacing humor is usually a good way to get an audience on your side, though some people think this devalues your authority—"and the hardest thing about going to conferences is actually applying these lessons in the real world. So I created a toolkit to help you with that, and it's super easy to get. I've compiled my PowerPoint slides, my notes and a couple of worksheets that will help you apply this to your unique situation. I've even included my bestselling ebook that goes in depth on how to apply these lessons. These are all available at justinblaney.com/landingpage." Use the name of the event for the name of your landing page to make it easy to remember. "Now you might be thinking, 'Great. This is where the speaker does a sales pitch for his crap.' However, I know you've already paid quite a bit for this event and I'm probably the worst salesperson in the history of speakers so I decided to make the whole thing free. Just go to justinblaney.com/landing page and download it now. I hope it's helpful for you. Thanks for listening and enjoy the rest of the conference!"

You can shorten this if you need to, or adapt it to your own style. The idea is to make your offer helpful, and helpful it should be. You're giving away a bunch of stuff that you worked hard to put together after all. Even asking for an email is an attempt to help them because you're not going to be spamming them, right? You're going to be emailing helpful insights on an ongoing basis. That's helpful. In addition to mentioning your URL from stage, you can print off cards to place on everyone's chair or table setting that has the web address and an explanation of what they get. That makes it easier for people to go online and get the resources. Whether or not you have a card, make sure that you show the URL on a screen. If you're just saying it and spelling it out loud, you'll miss a ton of potential leads.

One last way I've seen people get leads from speaking is passing around a basket that people can toss their business cards into in order to win a prize. A more sophisticated way to do this is to pass around iPads with an app that collects lead information. You have to give them some good reason to share their email, such as the prospect of winning something nifty, but many people will do it simply because everyone else is. No matter what approach you take, you can get a lot out of your speaking engagements if you take initiative and plan ahead. That hour you spend in front of them could be the most profitable hour you have all year.

APPLICATION FOR TODAY

Do you have a talk coming up? If not, spend a little time developing contacts with a chamber of commerce, networking group or local conference organizer. Once you have an engagement, spend some internal resources or hire someone to make a great landing page for you. Spend the time necessary to pull together the best resources you can to make the offer as enticing as possible. Even if you can't do that all today, make a list of the things you will need to do and get started on it now.

SEPARATION

What makes one person successful over another is a question that has been asked and answered, or at least attempted, by millions. Perhaps there are a million answers. Context certainly has something to do with it. It's hard for us to recreate what someone else has done if our context is completely different. Or even slightly different. One thing I've noticed about successful people is that they've managed to separate themselves from the masses. This is self-evident in a way. An NFL player is separated from the rest of us in the stands because their talent is higher than ours, but NFL players aren't born on the field. They're born in a hospital, usually, like most of us. Something between when they were born and their first NFL kickoff causes them to become NFL stars and us to sit in the stands. What happened? They found a way to separate themselves and they probably started young. They practiced harder. They spent more time in the weight room. They spent more time watching film. They studied the greats more carefully. They enjoyed the game a little more. Each of these areas is a little bit of separation that adds up to a big difference over time. I've noticed this in all areas of success. Highly successful people don't do things exactly like average-successful people. Some of it is natural ability, but I think part of that natural ability is a willingness to do things differently or to try a little harder. They find ways to separate themselves, whether consciously or not. They give better service, their quality is higher or their price is lower.

Something about super successful people has to be different or they'd be the

same as the rest of us.

I used to think artists were fakers, or at least oddballs. They would say things like, "I spent three weeks with a tribe in Africa, becoming one of their people without getting out my camera once. Then, when I was one of them, I began to capture their lives on film." I used to think that this was a bunch of filler in order to sound impressive. I've since noticed that the difference between a great photo and a masterpiece is in the small details. The smile on that girl in the photo is infinitesimally more genuine. The lines on that man's face are microscopically different and they reveal something about him that resonates just a little bit more. That's the difference between great and masterwork. Great artists do something to separate themselves from their peers and that's why they're great. Actors do things like carry their swords around for six weeks in order for it to feel like it belongs with them. Or they never break character during filming, even when they're home with their families. These strange things improve their performance in perhaps the slightest amount, but they've done something to separate themselves from their peers. And that's why they're great. The same is true with businesses. Great businesses do something to separate themselves from their competition. The start-ups that succeed over all the thousands that fail found some way to separate themselves from the others. They tweaked the recipe just a tiny bit and that made all the difference between failure and billionaire success.

You can't expect to perform better than your peers if you do exactly what they do. You have to find ways to separate yourself from them. That might be working longer hours, even if for only a few years until you build your advantage. That might be giving your customers extraordinary service. That might be coming up with a new way to get their products to them faster. The cool thing is that once you begin to separate yourself, it becomes harder for your peers to catch up. Over the course of a 30-year career, or even a 10-year run as a startup, you can become almost untouchable. How would you like to start an online book retailer today? Impossible to go up against Amazon, right? They've spent billions on delivering products faster and creating software that is easy to use and makes smart recommendations. But when they started they were just an ordinary shop online that spent the next 15 years separating themselves from their competition a little more each year. In fact, they rarely make money because they're reinvesting all their profits in continuing to create separation. They've become the biggest online retailer in the world and they're still not satisfied. That's probably a smart position, because in today's fast moving world a new start up could pop up that challenges their model if Amazon doesn't stay on top of those changes and use their resources to create that continuous separation.

What starts out as working a little harder or providing a

little better service eventually becomes an unfair advantage.

Your peers complain about how well you have it and wonder why you're so lucky, but you know that at one point you were equals. You were born in the same hospital, just like an NFL player and the rest of us sitting in the stands. Genes and talent have something to do with it. So do your parents, whether they're billionaires or just scraping by but loving and supportive. But when all else is equal, those who rise to the top find a way to separate themselves from everyone else a little bit each day until they become so successful everyone wonders how they got there.

APPLICATION FOR TODAY

What is one way you can separate yourself from your peers? Start doing that one thing today.

CLOSING

Who you are makes it easier to do what you do

Millions of people around the world could use your insights, your product, your vision for the world, your experience, your time. There's just one problem. They don't know you exist. Set out to help these people, one at a time at first, then more and more and more and one day you could stand back to realize you've become famous for your helpfulness.

You have been uniquely equipped to do something only you can do. This makes setting yourself apart easy. Easy in theory. First you have to cut through a lot of common misunderstandings and noise from people promising success in ten easy steps. You'll have to tear yourself away from the temptation to look at success and try hard to squeeze into somebody else's mold. Remember, great innovations tend to come from the freaks and geeks of the last era.

What you have to offer will not be found anywhere else and will not come from anybody else. This is your opportunity and yours alone. Just like you can't cram and stuff yourself into someone else's mold, to do what they do and think how they think and approach the world how they approach it, so nobody can cram themselves into your mold and operate the way you can. Embrace those things that make you different.

The world needs what you have to offer. Are you really going to deprive us all because nobody else is paving the way for you? Be a pioneer in helpfulness. Because someone who is famously helpful is never in want of customers, donors, jobs or friends — for all the right reasons.

Thank you for reading Famously Helpful

Have you seen these principles in action? If you have any stories that help illustrate the points made in this book, I'd love to hear from you. All other feedback is welcome too.

Email me at justin@justinblaney.com
Or connect @justinblaney
Your friend, Justin

Get a free download of Famously Helpful for Kindle or iPad

WWW.FAMOUSLYHELPFUL.COM

Made in the USA
Charleston, SC
23 November 2015